Disarmament and Demobilisation after Civil Wars

Contents

Oxford University Press, Walton Street, Oxford OX2 6DP
Oxford New York
Athens Auckland Bangkok Bombay
Calcutta Cape Town Dar es Salaam Delhi
Florence Hong Kong Istanbul Karachi
Kuala Lumpur Madras Madrid Melbourne
Mexico City Nairobi Paris Singapore
Taipei Tokyo Toronto
and associated companies in
Berlin Ibadan

Oxford is a trade mark of Oxford University Press

Published in the United States
by Oxford University Press Inc., New York

© The International Institute for Strategic Studies 1996

First published August 1996 by Oxford University Press for
The International Institute for Strategic Studies
23 Tavistock Street, London WC2E 7NQ

Director: Dr John Chipman
Deputy Director: Rose Gottemoeller

British Library Cataloguing in Publication Data

Data available

Library of Congress Cataloging in Publication Data

ISBN 0-19-828026-2
ISSN 0567-932X

GLOSSARY

ACABQ	Advisory Committee on Administrative and Budgetary Questions (UN)
ACC	Administrative Committee on Coordination (UN)
APLA	Azanian People's Liberation Army
BMATT	British Military and Assistance Training Team (Mozambique)
CAO	Chief Administrative Officer (UN)
CLO	Chief Logistics Officer (UN)
CMF	Commonwealth Monitoring Force (Zimbabwe)
CORE	Commission for the Reintegration of Demobilised Soldiers (Mozambique)
ECOMOG	ECOWAS peacekeeping force in Liberia
ECOWAS	Economic Community of West African States
EPLF	Eritrean People's Liberation Front
EPS	*Ejercito Popular Sandinista* (Nicaragua)
FADM	*Forcas Armadas de Defesa de Moçambique*
FAM	*Forcas Armadas de Moçambique*
FMLN	*Frente Farabundo Martí para la Liberación Nacional*
FRELIMO	*Frente Libertação de Moçambique*
ICRC	International Committee of the Red Cross
ILO	International Labour Organisation
IMF	International Monetary Fund
MICIVIH	Joint UN–OAS Civilian Mission to Haiti
MINUGUA	UN Mission for Guatemala
MK	*Umkhonto we Sizwe* (South Africa)
MPLA	*Movimento Popular para a Libertação de Angola*
NDC	National Demobilisation Commission (Somaliland)
NGO	non-governmental organisation
NRA	National Resistance Army (Uganda)
OAS	Organisation of American States
ONUCA	UN Observer Group in Central America
ONUSAL	United Nations Mission In El Salvador
PF	Patriotic Front (Zimbabwe)
PN	National Police (El Salvador)
PNC	National Civilian Police (El Salvador)
RENAMO	*Resistência Nacional Moçambicana*
RSF	Rhodesian Security Forces
SADF	South African Defence Force

SNA	Somali National Alliance
SNM	Somali National Movement
SOC	State of Cambodia
TBVC	Transkei, Bophuthatswana, Venda and Ciskei (South Africa)
UCAH	Humanitarian Assistance Coordination Unit (Angola)
UNAVEM	United Nations Angola Verification Mission
UNIDIR	United Nations Institute for Disarmament Research
UNITA	*União Nacional para a Independência Total de Angola*
UNITAF	Unified Task Force (Somalia)
UNOMIL	United Nations Observation Mission in Liberia
UNOSOM	United Nations Operation in Somalia
UNPA	United Nations Protected Areas (former Yugoslavia)
UNPROFOR	United Nations Protection Force (former Yugoslavia)
UNSCR	United Nations Security Council Resolution
UNTAC	United Nations Transitional Authority in Cambodia
URNG	*Unidad Revolucionaria Nacional Guatelmalteca*
USC	United Somali Congress
ZANLA	ZANU military wing
ZANU	Zimbabwe African Nationalist Union
ZAPU	Zimbabwe African People's Union
ZIPRA	ZAPU military wing

INTRODUCTION

Since 1989, international efforts to end protracted periods of conflict in parts of Africa, Central America and South-east Asia have all included initiatives and programmes to disarm and demobilise soldiers after years, often decades, of war and military service. While these initiatives have differed considerably in scope, they have all encompassed a number of complex steps which, in turn, have required financial and technical assistance from a range of outside actors. In each case, the basic goal has been a dual one: to reduce the size of the armed forces; while redefining their proper role in society alongside, although constitutionally and functionally separate from, the police and security forces. Where fighting has been inconclusive, the process has involved amalgamating formerly opposing armies in an attempt to forge new, legitimate and locally accepted structures. These objectives have also required provisions for reintegrating demobilised soldiers into civil society and productive economic life. In the long term, therefore, disarmament, demobilisation and reintegration could significantly reduce military expenditure, allowing scarce resources to be reallocated to social and developmental projects. In the short to medium term, however, arms and soldiers recently emerged from war are a potential source of domestic and regional instability. It is principally with this aspect that the present study is concerned.

The record of achievement in addressing the challenges outlined above has been highly uneven. The scale of such operations, the level of financial and political investment in them, and the probability that governments and international institutions will continue to face calls for involvement in this area, suggest that the precise nature of the issues involved deserves more systematic treatment than it has hitherto received.

This paper provides a framework for thinking about the proper place of disarmament, demobilisation and the reintegration of former combatants in settling internal armed conflicts. Its principal conclusion is that, as a set of distinct activities that require advance planning and outside assistance, these are all intensely political processes whose long-term and sustainable impact depend on parallel efforts of political and economic reconstruction to resolve, or ameliorate as far as possible, the root causes of conflict. Disarmament, demobilisation and reintegration cannot, in other words, be treated simply as a set of managerial or administrative challenges, as a number of institutions, non-governmental organisations (NGOs) and donors have been prone to do. To that extent, this paper accepts the view, forcefully expressed by Hans-Joachim Vergau with reference to the United Nations operation in Namibia in 1989, that 'one should not think that once a settlement has been agreed upon, implementation is a matter of technical arrangements'.[1] On the contrary, the record since 1989 clearly shows that 'those responsible for the planning and operational stages can and do affect confidence and trust, and therefore ultimately the acceptance of the settlement, by the way they approach their task'.[2] This study explores precisely how such 'confidence and trust' can be generated.

At the same time, very few of the parties to the armed conflicts examined in this paper have been able to claim complete victory at the end of armed hostilities. Where no party is victorious on the battlefield, the willingness of former enemies to set aside the military option in favour of a negotiated political settlement does not signify that all the factors that originally provoked and fuelled armed conflict have been addressed. Indeed, grievances and conflicts of interest, often of a fundamental nature, persist after the formal end of hostilities and, crucially, continue to exert a profound influence on the politics and process of 'peace-building'. It may be deeply misleading, therefore, to speak of 'comprehensive political settlements' or of conflicts as having been 'resolved' if by this it is understood that the formal end of armed hostilities also marks a definitive break with past patterns of conflict and violence. These considerations are key to understanding the challenges involved in designing disarmament, demobilisation and reintegration programmes. For such programmes to have a lasting impact, they must be part of a wider, long-term attempt to create the necessary political and psychological environment, as well as the necessary mechanisms and institutions, to address unresolved tensions without resorting to violence, thus helping to overcome the scars and complex legacies of war.

Scope of the Study
Chapter I considers the context in which disarmament, demobilisation and reintegration have taken place. It identifies three sets of circumstances:

• where disarmament and demobilisation provisions have been agreed among parties as part of an overall political settlement;

- where such provisions have been initiated by government or rebel forces that have achieved decisive victory in war; and
- where central authority has been too fragmented for a settlement to be reached and where the lack of nation-wide security has been deemed to require coercive action to disarm the warring factions.

Despite some important and obvious differences between these categories, the first chapter focuses above all on *common* features both directly and indirectly relevant to considerations of disarmament, demobilisation and reintegration. These features – whose intensity and importance vary greatly from case to case – derive from the intra-state character of conflict, the socio-economic legacy of protracted war, and the proliferation of arms in the countries and regions where disarmament and demobilisation have been attempted.

Chapters II and III concentrate on the particular challenges these features generate regarding disarmament and weapons control; demobilisation and the initial reintegration of ex-combatants; and the formation of new armed forces and national police forces.[3] These elements are closely linked and the activities associated with each phase should ideally be conceived of as a continuing and integrated process.

The final chapter, looking at the requirements for external support, coordination and financing of demobilisation and reintegration pro-grammes, considers why effective coordination has rarely been achieved in practice. It considers, in particular, the difficulties international organisations have encountered in attempting to integrate the activities of donors and, more generally, in designing programmes that take account of local institutions and capacities. Throughout the paper the analysis focuses primarily on the short to medium term: the initial disarmament and demobilisation of soldiers; and the transition to their participation in long-term reintegration programmes. The transition phase includes initial reintegration assistance provided to ex-combatants on demobilisation and the creation of unified armed forces and civilian police.

The reason for this focus on the short to medium term is twofold. First, in terms of security, as well as the underlying political fragility of a continuing peace process, the initial disarmament and demobilisation period is the most critical. If a process is derailed at this stage, measures aimed at long-term reintegration will be of little relevance. Second, as Alex Vines and João Coelho have observed regarding Mozambique, the broader process of reintegration is necessarily 'open ended in the sense that it tends to be merged with the socio-economic development of the country as a whole'.[4] A detailed study of the relationship between demobilisation and reintegration on the one hand, and economic and development issues on the other, is beyond the scope of this paper. Moreover, the empirical base on which to assess the long-term effect of various approaches to reintegration is still very limited. A study by the International Labour Organisation (ILO) in 1995 considers 2–3 years as a 'minimum period' for reintegration programmes 'to get under way', and 'another 3–5 years ... before the full impact of the programmes can be measured'.[5]

This is certainly not to underrate the critical importance of devoting attention and resources to the economic and social development of countries and regions that have experienced long periods of conflict. Indeed, an underlying theme throughout this paper is that *lasting* success in meeting the challenge of reintegrating arms and soldiers into society after an internal armed conflict depends largely on the extent to which short-term concerns about security and political stability are not only addressed, but also effectively reconciled with long-term strategies for economic reconstruction and development.[6]

I. THE CONTEXT

It has been observed that much of the recent writing on 'the state of peacekeeping offer[s] little or no systematic explanation of the features of recent conflicts that make peacekeeping so inherently difficult'.[1] This paucity is no doubt partly attributable to the exaggerated optimism that, in 1991 and 1992, characterised much of the public and academic debate about the 'unprecedented' possibilities offered by the end of East–West rivalry. Since late 1993, much of this optimism has been replaced by an understandable reluctance to make abstract and generalised assessments of the nature of post-Cold War conflict when its very diversity appears to defy such attempts.

Failure to explore the context and nature of contemporary conflict has, if anything, been more pronounced in policy-making circles where attention has tended to focus on short-term assistance rather than on the root causes and underlying characteristics of conflict. Although the reasons for this failure are varied and complex, it has adversely affected the quality of the assistance provided, particularly in those cases involving disarmament, demobilisation and reintegration. Only with a clearer appreciation of the context of such attempts at disarmament, demobilisation and reintegration can some of the 'features' that have made success so 'inherently difficult' be identified and their negative influence on a peace process be mitigated. As will be argued more fully later, while it is essential to recognise the uniqueness of individual conflicts and the variety of local actors and cultural settings that shape them, it is possible – and for conceptual and planning purposes necessary – to identify factors common, to a greater or lesser degree, to all or most of the cases where disarmament, demobilisation and reintegration of soldiers have been attempted. Moreover, the role of the armed forces in society following periods of internal conflict raises distinctive issues of its own.

Disarmament and Demobilisation Operations

Disarmament, demobilisation and reintegration efforts since 1989 fall broadly into three categories. Although not discrete or watertight, these categories provide useful conceptual distinctions for exploring both the technical and political challenges involved in specific cases, as well as some of their common features.

First, most large-scale efforts have been part of so-called 'comprehensive political settlements', agreed and negotiated under international – usually United Nations – auspices after years of inconclusive fighting between guerrilla and government forces. The UN operations in Namibia, Cambodia, Mozambique and El Salvador all grew out of such settlements and their successful implementation was firmly predicated on the continuing commitment of the parties to the original peace accords. In each of these cases, the UN and/or so-called 'friends' groups sought to 'institutionalise a framework for national reconciliation prior to full deployment of a UN peace operation'.[2] Negotiations currently under way in Guatemala between government representatives and rebel leaders of the *Unidad Revolucionaria Nacional Guatelmalteca* (URNG) are also aimed at reaching a peace agreement that will involve demobilisation and disarmament under UN auspices. In Angola, the attempt to disarm and demobilise government soldiers and forces of the *União Nacional para a Independência Total de Angola* (UNITA) by October 1992 was similarly conceived within the framework of a negotiated settlement.

In a second set of cases, responsibility for demobilisation and military reform has been assumed by governments victorious in civil war or otherwise not under direct military threat. The most comprehensive initiatives in this respect have occurred in Uganda, Ethiopia and Eritrea. In late 1992, Uganda began to reduce the size of the National Resistance Army (NRA) that had brought Yoweri Museveni to power in 1986. Over a period of three years and with financial support from the World Bank, the NRA has shed some 50,000 soldiers. By far the largest of all recent demobilisation efforts, however, has taken place in Ethiopia where an estimated 500,000 soldiers and officers of the previous Dergue regime (412,000 of whom were in rehabilitation camps) were demobilised in 1991.[3] Following the defeat of Mengistu Haile Mariam's army and the country's secession from Ethiopia in April 1993, Eritrea also initiated a demobilisation pro-gramme and has successfully reduced its 95,000-strong army by more than 50% in a two-phased programme. In 1993, the self-proclaimed Republic of Somaliland also initiated its own demobilisation programme. An estimated 30,000 fighters formerly of the Somali National Movement (SNM) are still to be demobilised.[4] A similar initiative carried out with French financial and technical assistance, but with only very modest results thus far, was initiated in Chad after the fall of Hissène Habré's regime in late 1990.

Finally, in a limited number of instances where political settlements have proved elusive – principally because the power and authority of the state have been too fragmented – outside forces have attempted to use coercion to facilitate disarmament and military reform. The UN's willingness to engage in 'coercive disarmament' in Somalia in 1993 was, at the time, considered a prerequisite for establishing the degree of security necessary to accomplish other tasks, specifically humanitarian relief and, more broadly, national reconciliation and economic reconstruction. Intervention in Somalia brought neither disarmament nor reconciliation to the country, yet the international involvement, especially in 1993, still merits close study. In part, this is because the broad background against which operations were carried out – the collapse or slow disintegration of authoritarian regimes from within, followed by an ineffectual attempt to restore central authority, the privatisation of the means of violence and the 'spread of non-state military formations'[5] – are, potentially at least, of much wider relevance.

As these categories are not watertight, the differences among the cases should not obscure the common elements and basic challenges that have been present in nearly all the conflicts where some form of disarmament, demobilisation and reintegration has been attempted. The impact of three sets of factors, in particular, merit more detailed discussion:

- Provisions for disarmament, demobilisation and reintegration have all been introduced in cases of intra-state conflict, most of which have also been characterised by elements of communal conflict.
- In all the cases examined, the prolonged experience of war and conflict has in itself helped to create an 'alternative' economic and social order. This has generated particular challenges for the demobilisation of soldiers and, above all, their effective reintegration into civilian life and their contribution to productive economic activity.
- The environment in which disarmament and demobilisation has taken place has been characterised by an abundance of arms and ammunition, especially small arms and light weapons.

Intra-state and Communal Conflict
All the major disarmament and demobilisation initiatives since 1989 have arisen from protracted periods of intra-state conflict in which 'identity-driven' or communal tensions have been prominent. In this context, the notion of communal conflict refers not only to inter-ethnic antagonism, with which it is sometimes equated, but also includes religious, linguistic and socio-economic divisions that serve, potentially,

as contributory factors or as sources of group identification in conflict. Writing in the early 1970s, Samuel Huntington identified three characteristics of communal conflict relevant to a broader understanding of intra-state conflict: their 'identity-driven' and polarised character; the high levels of violence involved; and their longevity. Although these characteristics are never present in equal measure, taken together they do much to explain why it is so difficult to generate the trust required if disarmament and demobilisation is to proceed.

Because communal conflict is perceived to involve 'fundamental questions of identity and the we–they distinction is clear-cut and overriding', it is characterised by a 'high degree of polarisation'.[6] The rise of ethno-nationalist conflict after the Cold War has highlighted the extreme difficulty of securing lasting settlements when issues of identity are involved. Attempts to define what actually constitutes a 'communal group', or indeed any other term used to describe aspects of contemporary conflict – most notably 'ethnic conflict', but also 'civil war' – are invariably both politically and conceptually contentious.[7] Indeed, as Adam Roberts perceptively notes, 'the words used to characterise a conflict ... often imply the type of interpretation to be placed on it', and a fundamental problem 'with all such terms is that they pigeon-hole conflicts that may have many dimensions'.[8] In their study of the multifaceted nature of the Angolan conflict, Rothchild and Hartzell note how the 'intrastate conflict [in Angola] has had personal, ideological, inter-ethnic, and inter-regional dimensions'.[9] In many cases, the 'ethnic' dimension of a conflict is difficult to separate from other elements. This is the case in Guatemala, whose 34-year war is rarely thought of in terms of ethnic conflict, although the brutal suppression of the Indian population was a key factor in the war's resurgence in the mid-1980s. Conflicts have also been particularly violent and seemingly irreconcilable among groups with similar ethnic roots. Perhaps the most frequently cited example is that of Somalia, whose recent history has been punctuated by periods of intense inter-clan fighting, but whose 'people' nevertheless possess a 'strong sense of ethnic exclusiveness in terms of language and culture'.[10]

Of principal concern here, however, is the perception of the nature of the conflict by the parties involved, and the extent to which these perceptions influence attitudes to, and the outcome of, disarmament, demobilisation and reintegration efforts. While perceptions of communal identity that give rise to or reinforce conflict may be 'imagined' and correspond poorly, if at all, to anthropological data, they are still nevertheless genuinely felt. Moreover, even though 'ethnic groups' are rarely homogenous, where wars have been fought over a considerable period of time, the socialising effect of participating in a common struggle, often combined with a conscious effort to mobilise soldiers along ethnic lines, ensures that a conflict itself effectively becomes communalised. As John Markakis has noted regarding the 'ethnic factor' in the Horn of Africa, 'identity is itself defined in the process of interaction – cooperation, competition, confrontation, even war – among groups'.[11]

A second characteristic of communal conflicts identified by Huntington is that they 'typically involve large amounts of violence and often particularly vicious forms of violence'.[12] This is often cited as a general feature of civil wars. It is certainly the case that contemporary conflicts in which demobilisation and military reform have become the object of negotiations between the parties involved have been characterised by exceptional savagery and persistent human-rights violations. In Angola, an estimated 300,000 people have died since the resumption of civil war in late 1992. Since the armed struggle began in El Salvador in the late 1970s, nearly 100,000 people have died while another one million – out of a population of just under five million – have become refugees or internally displaced. Liberia's collapse into civil war in 1989 has, by some estimates, resulted in the death of one-tenth of the population. The scale and nature of violence in intra-state conflict have a direct bearing on disarmament and demobilisation efforts in two respects. First, and most obviously, confidence and mutual trust between parties are necessarily more difficult to generate and far more susceptible to reversal and rapid erosion when violence has been acute, indiscriminate and widespread. Second, more often than not the armed forces to be 'reformed' as part of a settlement have, in the past, been the instruments of state repression and violence. For example, the death squads responsible for the disappearances, massacres and 'extra-judicial' executions in El Salvador throughout the 1980s were effectively immune from prosecution, even though the central role of the military in this wave of repression is now indisputable.[13] A similar pattern is found in Guatemala and Haiti. In South Africa, the former South African Defence Force (SADF), as one observer put it, 'allowed itself to be used for improper or unprofessional purposes'.[14] In all these circumstances, the integration or creation of new armed and police forces requires more than simple institutional reform, and the 'professionalisation' of the armed forces must involve more than the acknowledgement of past human-rights abuses. As will be argued below, only a long-term and sustained effort can overcome the legacy of violence and establish legitimate structures that inspire public confidence.

Huntington's third characteristic relates to the fact that intra-state conflicts often last a long time. In Angola, armed conflict began in the early 1960s, first against Portuguese colonial rule and later, once independence had been granted, between the *Movimento Popular para a Libertação de Angola* (MPLA) and UNITA. From the 1960s until the peace accord was signed in October 1992, Mozambique – with Angola the most impoverished and long-suffering war zone of sub-Saharan Africa – displayed a similar pattern of almost uninterrupted warfare. In Guatemala, where a peace agreement has yet to be reached between rebel forces and the government, fighting has lasted for 35 years.

The longevity of conflicts influences demobilisation and reintegration efforts in a variety of ways. On the one hand, the destruction of national infrastructure, the drain on human capital, the very substantial movements of refugees and internally displaced peoples and the weakening of public-sector institutions by extended periods of fighting, all add to the logistical and technical challenges involved in organising and sustaining demobilisation and reintegration programmes. On the other hand, expectations among ordinary soldiers about the implications of peace for employment and increased welfare are usually high when most, sometimes all, of their adult lives have been spent on the battlefield. Such expectations in turn put pressure on leaders to deliver at the negotiating table and reduce the scope for compromise agreements. But the longevity and legacy of war also have more profound economic and social implications which not only complicate the transition to peace, but can also make the very prospect of demobilisation and surrendering weapons appear less attractive than continued fighting.

War as 'Social Order' and the Transition to Peace
War structures both the economic and social life of the society in which it takes place in profound ways. Over time, it becomes a social and economic order that benefits certain groups and interests, but leaves others permanently disadvantaged. The political and security considerations with which this paper is primarily concerned cannot, therefore, be separated from the social and economic consequences that the prospect

of disarmament, demobilisation and the 'outbreak of peace' entail for various groups and interests in society. 'Part of the problem', as David Keen perceptively observes, 'is that we tend to regard conflict as, simply, a breakdown in a particular system, rather than as the emergence of another, alternative system of profit and power'.[15] Viewed as an 'alternative system', war and organised violence can powerfully benefit certain groups and interests while a transition to peace is likely adversely to affect their privileged status. In a study of the 'grass-roots war economy' in parts of Mozambique during the civil war, Mark Chingono found that 'illegal crossborder trade flows from Zimbabwe to Manica Province and further to Beira provided a major stimulus to sustained economic expansion, social differentiation and shifts in power bases'.[16] He notes further that even the 'collapse of state power removed some of the traditional obstacles to change, and gave rise to a new entrepreneurial class (of bureaucratic entrepreneurs, artisans, money dealers, smugglers, pirates, racketeers, barefoot traders etc.)'. Central to the present study is the implication that comes from this, namely, that 'any post-peace reconstruction programme will to a large extent be influenced by the operation of the grass-roots war-economy', and that policies, including those related to demobilisation and reintegration, must be 'sensitive to the needs of various social groups'.[17] In addition to the economic and social impact on various groups, transitions to peace involve complex individual choices and dilemmas for combatants preparing for civilian life. These considerations have only marginally, if at all, influenced the design of demobilisation and reintegration programmes.

The economic interests that have obstructed demobilisation and reintegration are sometimes very direct and well documented. In Angola, one of the richest countries anywhere in terms of natural resources, UNITA has been able to prosecute the war and pay its fighters because it controls diamond-rich provinces in the north of the country; specifically the Cuango valley which accounts for an estimated 80% of Angola's total output. The eruption of fighting between government forces and UNITA in August 1995 resulted from an attempt to frustrate UNITA's diamond operations in the north. Similarly, the importance for Cambodia's Khmer Rouge – which chose not to disarm or demobilise its forces as agreed under the peace accords signed in Paris in October 1991 – of cross-border smuggling in timber and gems along the border with Thailand, and the collusion of the Thai military, is also well documented.

In parts of Central America, problems of demobilisation and reintegration have been directly linked to the issue of land redistribution and the terms of land ownership intended to benefit ex-combatants. Indeed, the failure to implement land transfer schemes in El Salvador is currently the most serious threat to the fragile stability that has been achieved there. Some three years after the peace agreement was signed, social tensions rose as nearly 40% of former *Frente Farabundo Martí para la Liberación Nacional* (FMLN) fighters were still waiting for land.[18] While the delay was partly the result, as the government claimed, of an initially lacklustre response from the donor community, this issue of land is clearly perceived by the landed interests – with which the military and various paramilitary groups have traditionally been associated – as destabilising to social order and a threat to their economically privileged position. Similarly, 'socio-economic and agrarian topics' are the principal stumbling blocs to peace between the URNG and the government in Guatemala. There, the Army, 'always ... the power behind the throne' of the regime, considers its extensive privileges to be under threat.[19] Such 'privileges' include not only extraordinary political influence, freedom from civilian oversight and effective immunity from prosecution for human-rights violations, but also amassing personal wealth. In El Salvador, military involvement in organised criminal activity, tolerated under previous regimes, is now clearly 'threatened' by the onset of peace and the creation of new police forces.[20] Experiences in Central America since 1991 show, not surprisingly, that settlements involving the exchange or promise of land are invariably politically and socially more complex since they touch directly on issues related to the very structure of the society concerned. Indeed, as Alvaro de Soto, a key figure in the UN's involvement in the region since the late 1980s, has observed: 'by addressing land the Chapultepec agreement took on an issue that had been at the core of Salvadoren tensions since colonial times'.[21]

Economic considerations can also have a very direct bearing on the individual decisions of soldiers and officers weighing the option of demobilisation and reintegration. Where, as in parts of Africa, economic incentives have become primary motives for fighting, such considerations will be pre-eminent in decisions of whether to disarm or retain weapons and continue fighting. As Alex de Waal has noted, 'for a significant number of men in Africa, fighting is a way of life itself: a career, a profession, even a vocation', while 'the war aims of more and more insurgents and militias are more and more local and specific ...

Sustaining and enriching themselves ... have become the overriding preoccupation of some groups'.[22] According to one relief official in Somalia, 'the lack of alternative means of survival for the people of Somalia encourages participation in militias', including 'freelance' militias with 'no strong commitment to a specific party' whose chief motivation for armed struggle is largely, if not exclusively, economic.[23] Similarly, a study of child soldiers in Liberia recently observed how armed groups 'stranded in the capital without family or community support' had little incentive to demobilise without basic food security.[24] When institutionalised law and order is weakened by war and economic decline, both organised and random criminal activity increase and looting, extortion and robbery become principal sources of income. Indeed, Keen argues that in parts of Africa 'war itself has become privatised' as 'financially strapped governments – faced with pressure for austerity from international creditors – have tried to cut costs and reward supporters by delegating, in effect, the right to inflict violence and obtain loot'.[25]

While such cases may be extreme, an important implication for disarmament, demobilisation and reintegration activities is that weapons always have an *economic* as well as a *security* value for those who possess them. With limited employment opportunities and few marketable skills among soldiers, this in itself is a disincentive to lay down arms.

The longevity of conflict also means that army life and the social networks that have evolved around it are the only ones with which combatants are truly familiar. Although the regimentation and hardships attendant on army life may be deeply resented, any adjustment from military to civilian life poses particular problems when professional qualifications are lacking and educational and retraining programmes are limited. Exchanging the security of military life for the uncertainty of civilian life also involves socio-psychological adjustments with which ex-combatants have often been ill-equipped to cope. When soldiers have been fighting for all or most of their lives, the non-military skills acquired will be correspondingly small and adjustment, in the broadest sense, will be particularly hard.

The extent to which these considerations – economic ones related to the possession of arms and, more generally, a reluctance to abandon a way of life which, however miserable, offers a measure of socio-psychological security – adversely affect disarmament and demobilisation varies considerably from case to case. Nevertheless, in the short to medium term, the general willingness to abandon weapons and enter civilian life depends, principally, on the extent to which the security environment and the viability of continuing political processes are perceived to be taking root. In the long term, social and economic progress, reflected in increased job opportunities, food security and welfare provisions, are the decisive factors.

Abundance and Proliferation of Arms

A third factor affecting disarmament and demobilisation efforts is the abundance of arms in the countries concerned and the ease with which small arms and light weapons can be obtained locally and/or on the world market. According to one estimate, light weapons were responsible for over 90% of the deaths and injuries in the 90 armed conflicts in progress in 1993.[26] For this reason, above all, efforts at disarmament and weapons control have concentrated on this category of weapons. The precise definition of 'light weapons', however, is subject to debate. It is understood here to subsume 'small arms' and to include weapons ranging from assault rifles to anti-tank weapons (e.g., RPG-7, M-72) and light anti-aircraft systems (e.g., *Stinger*, SAM-7 and RBS-70).[27]

The challenges of disarmament and weapons control since 1989 have been formidable, requiring significant logistical and financial commitments by the outside actors or agencies engaged in the process. The UN Transitional Authority in Cambodia (UNTAC) is reported to have taken possession of 300,000 weapons and 80 million rounds of ammunition.[28] Although impossible to verify, it has been estimated that the *Frente Libertação de Moçambique* (FRELIMO) government distributed an estimated one million AK-47 rifles to civilian 'self-defence units' in Mozambique in the 1980s and that a much higher figure remains 'unaccounted for', even after the end of the United Nations operation, ONUMOZ.[29] In Angola, Somalia, Liberia and Central America, where disarmament initiatives have all been undertaken, very substantial quantities of weapons and ammunition have been accumulated and remain hidden throughout the countryside. While many of these weapons date from the Cold War, there is little evidence to suggest that the supply of small and light weapons is drying up. On the contrary, the problem of proliferation has become more acute and, arguably, less controllable since 1989.[30] Three factors merit special attention in this regard.

First, and most generally, the manufacture of, and international trade in, small arms remain highly decentralised, offering a range of potential suppliers and constant downward pressure on prices. Nearly 300 companies in more than 50 countries are 'actively manufacturing small arms, equipment and accessories'.[31] The degree of decentralisation is particularly pronounced in certain categories of weapons, most notably land-mines where an estimated 5–10 million anti-personnel mines are manufactured annually by some 100 private and state-owned companies.[32] The proliferation and widespread distribution of land-mines, whose lethal character is not diminished by the end of hostilities, has proved a particularly sinister obstacle to the effective reintegration of ex-soldiers and their dependants after conflict. An estimated 26,000 casualties are claimed by land-mines every year. In countries such as Cambodia, Angola and Mozambique, indiscriminate use of mines has left an additional legacy with a direct bearing on reintegration: large tracts of land polluted by mines have been rendered unusable for agricultural activity. During conflicts, mines are also typically laid in irrigation or water-delivery systems, in power plants, on paths and roads, as well as near and around national infrastructure facilities.[33] All this undermines economic reconstruction at the local, community-based level where attempts to reintegrate ex-combatants have been relatively successful. Still, attempts to regulate, let alone ban, the production and trade in mines have met with little success, as have attempts to control the trade in light weapons.

Second, the collapse of the Soviet Union in 1991 and the absence of any effective export-control mechanisms in former Soviet republics where light-weapon manufacturing has been extensive (Russia, Belarus, Ukraine and Georgia) resulted, in the early 1990s, in a 'sudden availability of massive amounts of new and surplus light weapons', much of which has resurfaced in areas of communal and regional conflict.[34] The breakdown in governmental control of this trade has been compounded by a 'significant increase in illicit sales of light weapons by newly privatised or decontrolled arms firms ... with a very substantial flow of firearms into black-market channels'.[35] At the same time, in parts of Armenia, Georgia and Azerbaijan, communal conflicts and wars have been sustained by a plentiful supply of equipment and ammunition from the former Soviet armed forces.

Third, large quantities of surplus weapons from past conflicts make their way to zones of conflict through a growing network of semi-official and secret arms pipelines. Where stockpiles of weapons exist after extended periods of conflict, re-exporting 'surplus weapons' is a temptation that can be difficult to resist for governments short of revenue and anxious to accelerate economic reconstruction. According to one study, an 'escalating number of such weapons are getting into the hands of an increasing number of soldiers, paramilitary forces, non-state actors and civilians involved in ethnic conflicts'.[36] For example, in spite of the embargo that used to operate in the former Yugoslavia, significant amounts of light weapons were obtained for Bosnia from surplus stocks in Lebanon. Similarly Ethiopia, under Mengistu Haile Mariam, received large quantities of arms from the Soviet Union (especially in 1977–85), and much of the surplus stock from what was once Africa's largest army is now used to supply, through a variety of channels, willing buyers elsewhere on the continent. A lasting and disturbing legacy of the Afghan war in the 1980s was the amount of arms delivered by the Soviet Union and the United States to their respective clients: the embattled government; and the *mujaheddin* resistance.[37] Not only did this leave the region with an unknown number of arms caches, but the US–Pakistani arms pipeline established during the war 'leaked' enormous quantities of weapons. Indeed, Afghanistan and the eastern seaboard of Africa are assumed to house two of the most organised post-Cold War arms pipelines. According to one study by the United Nations Institute for Disarmament Research (UNIDIR), 'there is no phenomenon in international trade in major weapons that can be compared to the leaking, rupturing and continuing pipelines of small arms'.[38] Because these weapons usually resurface in areas of continuing conflict involving non-state actors, the export channels tend to be private, semi-official and clandestine, adding further to the problem of regulation.[39]

The transnational nature of the illegal trade in light weapons and the relative ease with which these weapons can be acquired, strongly suggest that regional support is essential to the long-term effectiveness of disarmament and arms-control efforts within a given conflict area. Even if borders are not perfectly sealed, a genuine regional commitment to the peace process can have an important impact. As David Cox has observed with respect to Central America, a 'strong regional consensus in support of disarmament' meant that 'border monitoring, while not perfect, was adequate because the traffic in arms was restricted by the powers with the ability to restrict it'.[40] By contrast, arms embargoes against the former Yugoslavia and Somalia did very little to stop the traffic in arms.

'Comprehensive Settlements' or Unfinished Civil Wars?
Clearly, where a government controls its territory after victory on the battlefield it can impose conditions on membership of the armed forces and set the timetable for demobilisation. And it does not have to fear that

a disarmament process will alter the balance of military power to its disadvantage. By contrast, the consent and cooperation of the parties concerned is likely to be fragmented and incomplete where political authority is diffused and central institutions weak. Yet this chapter has also highlighted some features common to the various case-studies. At a practical level, the problems of reintegrating ex-combatants into the productive life of the country and the disposal of surplus weapons still have to be addressed in cases such as Ethiopia and Eritrea. But more fundamentally, where a settlement has been agreed between parties, the subsequent challenges of disarmament and nation-wide security have often differed less than expected from those cases where central authority is severely weakened and fragmented. Indeed, the above considerations strongly suggest that while a 'comprehensive political settlement' may have been agreed on paper, it should be taken into account when planning for disarmament, demobilisation and the initial period of reintegration that what is being dealt with are in many ways unfinished civil wars. This highlights the need for strategies that reflect the state of political relations between the conflicting parties as opposed to extraneous considerations and inflexible timetables for implementation. Indeed, the outcome of any demobilisation and reintegration programme depends first and foremost on the political context in which it is carried out and the extent to which divisions and animosities generated by years of war have been overcome or sufficiently attenuated by negotiations. While the precise relationship between the political context and the process of demobilisation varies from country to country, political will among the parties involved remains the chief criterion for success.

In the absence of political trust and a basic willingness to abide by agreements already entered into, demobilisation programmes are likely to fail, however well they are designed and financed. The Khmer Rouge's refusal to adhere to the Paris agreement of October 1991 and the obstruction and intimidation of the State of Cambodia (SOC) were the chief reasons for UNTAC's failure to demobilise the four factions in Cambodia. Similarly, commenting on the delays in the demobilisation and reintegration of some 60,000 soldiers in Liberia, UN Secretary-General Boutros Boutros-Ghali stressed that 'mistrust, lack of commitment and, in some instances, open hostility between and among various parties and other armed groups have been and continue to be the principal reasons for the slow pace of disarmament'.[41] By contrast, once the long-term viability of a peace process has been accepted and internalised by conflicting parties, obstacles hitherto thought insurmountable lose much of their obstructive potential. As Cox notes with respect to the less-than-truly effective disarmament of the Nicaraguan Contras by the UN Observer Group in Central America (ONUCA) in 1990: 'Whether or not weapons [belonging to the Contras] were concealed ... was not a critical matter as long as the outcome of the disarmament process was *politically credible* and acceptable to all parties'.[42]

It should also be recognised that in cases where neither side has 'won', the fundamental roots of the conflict remain unresolved. With regard to El Salvador, de Soto and del Castillo recognise that 'the problem of land was as much a root cause of the armed conflict that raged throughout the 1980s as was the overbearing power of the armed forces'.[43] Yet they also acknowledge that the peace agreement reached at Chapultepec in January 1992 was 'not an attempt at land reform or a mechanism for income distribution'.[44] While the delays in implementing the peace accord since 1992 owe much to genuine bureaucratic obstacles, it is difficult to dissociate these delays (let alone the long-term viability of the peace accords) altogether from the aforementioned facts.

The case of Angola also shows that a peace accord in itself does not guarantee success, and that the institutional arrangements set up under the accords to support disarmament and demobilisation need to reflect realities on the ground. Margaret Anstee, the Special Representative of the Secretary-General in Angola during the ill-fated UN Angola Verification Mission (UNAVEM II) in 1991–93, put the issue bluntly: 'the [peace] accords relied on a kind of "Boy Scouts" honour in a situation which had not exactly been conducive to the development of the Boy Scout spirit'.[45] Even in Mozambique, where many of the lessons from Angola had been absorbed, the Special Representative of the Secretary-General, Aldo Ajello, felt that problems encountered during implementation were 'mainly due to a lack of provisions for confidence-building and reconciliation measures in the Peace Agreement'.[46] These, he noted, included the absence of 'provision for monitoring the police' and 'a neutral body assuring impartial governance in the transitional period [and] a power-sharing arrangement for the period after elections'.[47] It was precisely over disarmament and demobilisation that such deficiencies manifested themselves most clearly and, in the case of Angola, with such fateful consequences.

A further and final consideration concerns the relationship between the end of the Cold War and prospects for resolving internal conflict. Immediately following the multi-party elections in Angola in September

1992, Herman Cohen, US Assistant Secretary of State for African Affairs under President George Bush, informed a Congressional committee of the US insistence that the UN operation in Mozambique be 'a lean one, based on the Angolan example'.[48] Cohen's unfortunate remark is interesting because it echoes a sentiment widespread in both policy-making and academic circles between 1988 and the UN Security Council summit in New York in January 1992. It was widely assumed that many internal and regional conflicts, such as those in Cambodia, Angola, Mozambique and Central America, had been sustained largely by the dynamics of Cold War confrontation. Thus, divorcing them from the pattern of global confrontation would lead to accommodation and lasting political settlements. The settlements reached in Paris, Bicesse and Rome to provide 'comprehensive political solutions' to conflicts in Cambodia, Angola and Mozambique respectively were all predicated, if only implicitly, on this assumption. When conflicts did not end, it was because they also involved local, often communal elements, many of which were themselves distorted, brought to the fore and exacerbated by Cold War rivalry. This, together with the abundance of weapons and techniques learned from previous patrons, explains in part why conflicts have continued (and even intensified), even though they no longer serve as objects of global competition. While this clearly suggests that the degree to which internal conflicts are amenable to external manipulation should not be overestimated, the discussion in the following chapters also shows that poorly planned, ill-coordinated and inadequately funded programmes can exacerbate the political tensions that inevitably characterise any post-conflict situation.

II. DISARMAMENT, WEAPONS CONTROL AND SECURITY

This chapter examines the role of disarmament and weapons control in conflict resolution and, more specifically, their importance as preliminary steps towards demobilising and reintegrating ex-combatants and amalgamating opposing armies. Although these activities usually overlap in time, establishing a 'secure environment' is a necessary first step without which the other activities cannot be implemented. There is, however, no automatic or inherent relationship between the process of disarmament and the creation of a secure environment. How and by what means such an environment is established is the central challenge. Although the continuing presence of arms is clearly part of that challenge, disarmament in the strict sense of eradicating or permanently removing the means of violence is not, for reasons that will be explored, a credible option in the short to medium term. Indeed, under certain circumstances, disarmament is likely to aggravate rather than enhance the security required for demobilisation and reintegration to proceed without the overwhelming risk of sudden break-down and reversal.

Coercion versus Consent-Based Approaches
Integral to any demobilisation programme is the need to establish a safe environment in which to carry out operations and prepare the ground for reintegration schemes. The abundance of arms and munitions in war-ridden countries is always a potential security problem, especially for civilian agencies engaged in relief and/or development work. This challenge can, in theory, be met either by disarming factions completely or, less ambitiously, by instituting various forms of weapons control. In either case, a coercive approach – the use, or threat, of force to compel disarmament – has received much attention from policy-makers and defence analysts since 1991–92. The issue of coercive disarmament arises, above all, where private and irregular units and formations threaten the security of operations. It has also been argued that some form of disarmament is the only effective response to the problem of surplus weapons accumulated over years of conflict. Much of this surplus was generously provided by external patrons during the Cold War, and is now frequently re-exported into areas of conflict.

The second United Nations Operation in Somalia (UNOSOM II), established in early May 1993, explicitly incorporated the option of coercive disarmament in its mandate and is therefore of particular interest to any discussion about using force in disarmament and weapons control.[1] While it may be argued that force was used or mandated – at least initially – only to secure humanitarian relief deliveries, the 'disarmament concept' for Somalia developed in the course of *Operation Restore Hope* (9 December 1992–4 May 1993) and which UNOSOM II sought to implement clearly envisaged the need for forcible disarmament.[2] For this reason, the problem of arms in Somalia in 1992–93 and the ill-fated attempts to address it, are of much more general interest.

The experience of Somalia, however, needs to be evaluated in relation to other essentially consent-based approaches to disarmament attempted in Liberia, Angola, Mozambique and Nicaragua. Furthermore, the largely ill-fated efforts to disarm factions and control certain categories of weapons held by belligerents in the former Yugoslavia – in the UN Protected Areas (UNPAs) in Croatia in 1992; in the 'safe area' of Srebrenica in April 1993; and around Sarajevo in 1994 – also shed light on the role and place of such attempts in the midst of a continuing conflict.[3] Together, these cases help to illustrate the relationship between disarmament and security in intra-state conflict.[4]

The Problem of Arms in Somalia, 1992–93
Using coercive methods to disarm parties on the ground in Somalia first arose with *Operation Restore Hope*, when a US-led multinational Unified Task Force (UNITAF) was authorised by the UN Security Council to make 'use of all necessary means to establish as soon as possible a secure environment for humanitarian relief operations in Somalia'.[5] UNITAF, set up under Chapter VII of the UN Charter, was established with reference to one of five options outlined by the Secretary-General in late November 1992 – the other four were drafted with a view to their likely rejection by the Security Council – to establish 'conditions for the uninterrupted delivery of relief supplies to the starving people of Somalia'.[6] The accepted option called for 'a country-wide enforcement operation undertaken by a group of member states authorised to do so by the Security Council'.[7] UNITAF did not, however pursue a vigorous or comprehensive disarmament policy.[8] Indeed, the extent to which disarmament should be undertaken systematically in the north and south of the country became a subject of public disagreement between US authorities and the newly appointed UN Secretary-General, Boutros-Ghali, who personally favoured a forceful approach to disarmament. The precise meanings of 'secure environment' and 'all necessary means' for disarmament – key phrases

used both in the US Central Command mission statement and the UN enabling resolution (UNSCR 794) – inevitably lend themselves to different interpretations. It is clear, however, from statements by President Bush and the UNITAF Commander at the time, Lieutenant-General Robert Johnston, that the US perceived its objectives in limited terms: to end starvation by protecting food and medical convoys sent to famine areas; to provide security in the 'hardest-hit areas'; and to prepare to turn the operation over to a UN force. The UN Secretary-General, on the other hand, embraced a more comprehensive concept of disarmament, and disagreements over the issue delayed the transfer of UNITAF functions to UNOSOM II.[9] In the end, UNITAF did not attempt a comprehensive disarmament policy, although it did institute various weapons-control measures and engaged in partial disarmament efforts. On 12 January 1993, for example, US forces seized 900 weapons including crew-served anti-tank weapons and small arms. Such efforts nevertheless remained patchy in scope, poorly organised and confused in implementation.[10]

Partly for this reason, Somalia's humanitarian situation in early 1993, although vastly improved compared to the previous summer, remained precarious. The abundance of weapons and the general state of anarchy that still characterised many aspects of Somali society led the Security Council to approve a UN implementation plan in March 1993 under which UNOSOM II 'would seek to complete, through disarmament and reconciliation, the task begun by UNITAF for the restoration of peace, stability, law and order'.[11] Consequently, UNOSOM II was 'endowed with enforcement powers under Chapter VII of the Charter' and became the 'first operation of its kind to be authorised by the international community'.[12] The authorising resolution stressed the 'fundamental importance of a *comprehensive* and effective programme for disarming Somali *parties*, including *movements* and *factions*'.[13] The Commission of Inquiry set up by the Security Council in February 1994 to investigate the armed attacks on UNOSOM personnel clearly stated in its final report that 'unlike UNITAF, whose participation in the disarmament process was subsidiary and derived from the ceasefire and disarmament agreements of 8 and 15 January 1993, the new UNOSOM was mandated to disarm militias'.[14]

Significantly, however, the 'mandate would also empower UNOSOM II to provide assistance to the Somali people in rebuilding their shattered economy and social and political life, re-establishing the country's constitutional structure, achieving national reconciliation, [and] recreating a Somali State based on democratic governance'.[15] And yet, as the Commission Report noted, 'enforcement power did not extend to Somalia's political process' where the mandate was to assist the 'Somalis in their efforts to achieve national reconciliation and reconstitution of their political institutions'.[16] These were ambitious goals, indeed; yet they highlighted the overall context and underlying long-term rationale for international involvement in Somalia. In authorising the task force in December 1992, when the emergency needs were paramount, Boutros-Ghali had already stressed that creating conditions for the 'uninterrupted delivery of relief supplies' was 'only part, albeit the most urgent, of the problem in Somalia and efforts [were] also required to create the *political conditions* in which Somalia can begin to resolve its political problem and rehabilitate its economy'.[17] It is in relation to this context that the specific objective of disarmament and the modalities by which it would be accomplished must be examined. What can safely be said is that none of these objectives could have been achieved without the support of the Somalis themselves, and that any attempt to disarm armed factions would have to be complemented by initiatives aimed at building local support and confidence in the peace process.

It has been argued, not least by the UN Secretary-General himself, that UNITAF's failure to engage in 'country-wide enforcement' and disarm factions was a 'lost opportunity'.[18] While there is little doubt that a more sustained effort could have been initiated, three closely related factors – evident in other operations and therefore relevant to disarmament policies more broadly – suggest that even with a more forceful disarmament policy in late 1992 and early 1993 the long-term security and political situation may not have improved appreciably:

- the sheer scale of the weapons problem and the consequent dangers of partial and incomplete disarmament when underlying political stability remains acutely fragile;
- the absence of a political strategy to underpin disarmament efforts;
- limited or 'soft' political will among outside actors to persist with coercive tactics, especially when casualties are likely to be sustained.

These factors represent, in much-distilled form, the principal lessons of Somalia and, as will be seen, are also relevant to explicitly consent-based disarmament and weapons-control policies.

Destabilising Consequences of Partial Disarmament
Even if the UNITAF programmes to eliminate weapons had been more forceful, there may simply have been too many weapons in circulation for these to have been effective given both the time and geographic constraints imposed by UNITAF. In a recent study of the forms of constitutional government that may be appropriate for Somalis, a leading authority on Somali society notes how 'today, almost every male has an automatic rifle, and some have even heavier weapons, which constitute a serious obstacle to the formation of governmental structures'.[19] Moreover, as noted in Chapter I, the manufacture of and trade in light weapons is notoriously difficult to control. Not only are illicit transactions more easily concealed and the range of suppliers much greater than for heavier categories of weapons, but the 'supplier–client–user relationship' is more complex and, according to UNIDIR, a 'sizeable share of small arms deals are increasingly between private individuals, sub-national groups or non-state actors who also act as conduits for actual users'.[20] Given UNITAF's brief and self-imposed time-frame, the scope for effective disarmament would have been severely limited, even if conditions had been more orderly on the ground.

In terms of geographic constraints, UNITAF's attempts to create a 'secure environment' were confined to parts of southern Somalia and a bias in favour of urban areas meant that many weapons were simply moved to the interior. It has nevertheless been argued that some disarmament is better than none. But this view fails to take into account the dynamics of conflicts with a multiplicity of armed parties and a tense political situation. Indeed, in conditions of real or latent civil war, partial disarmament can be potentially destabilising. The reason for this is simple: when conditions on the ground are fluid, central authority weak and country-wide security correspondingly lacking, the 'peace and reconciliation process' is highly vulnerable to changes in local allegiances, as well as to any shift in the balance of external forces. Somalia is only one example that suggests that under such circumstances the local impact of disarmament initiatives may hinder the creation of a 'secure environment'. As Clement Adibe observes in an admirable study of the disarmament component of the various phases of international involvement in Somalia:

> The general consequence of embarking on disarmament in fits and starts was that the entire programme had the effect of punishing those compliant segments of the population, some of whom fell

victim to gangs because they had been dispossessed of their weapons in areas where disarmament had been implemented by UN troops before the commander was replaced, or in areas where UN troops were ordered to pull out or the programme was scrapped entirely.[21]

Mohamed Sahnoun, reflecting on developments in Somalia after his abrupt departure as UN Special Representative in late 1992, also observed how the 'decision to disarm one clan, but not all clans at the same time, was a recipe for continuous civil war in the country'.[22] And as John Drysdale has observed, the case of the self-proclaimed Republic of Somaliland (where no foreign troops were deployed) shows that the 'establishment of a secure environment among Somali communities, including disarmament, is not a function of foreign deterrence. It is a function of Somali politics'.[23] The adverse impact of a 'fits-and-starts' policy on the security situation is likely to be particularly pronounced if disarmament measures are forcibly implemented where tensions run high and conflicts are still very much unresolved. An internal and widely circulated White Paper on the lessons of Somalia produced by the US Army–Air Force Center for Low Intensity Conflict in February 1994, tellingly observed that 'an un-quantifiable factor in maintaining force security [during the UNITAF phase] was the tone of the political–diplomatic measures undertaken during this period'.

The potentially destabilising consequences of partial and incomplete disarmament have also been demonstrated elsewhere, notably in Liberia where a detailed report of the Economic Community of West African States (ECOWAS) peacekeeping force in Liberia (ECOMOG) and the UN Observation Mission in Liberia (UNOMIL) activities in the course of 1994 found that:

> As a rule disarmament planners should not attempt to disarm factions until they have organised effective state wide security or at least the guarantee of achieving it. In the uncertain period after the reduction of hostilities, a failed or half successful disarmament can encourage a proliferation of smaller groups at local level.[24]

The Liberian experience 'demonstrated that some UN officials and internationally respected diplomats involved in designing and negotiating the peace process cherished an academic perception of the value of disarmament per se'.[25]

The observation applies with equal force to other operations. According to Ekwall-Uebelhart and Raevsky, the key lesson of the hapless record of local disarmament initiatives during the UN Protection Force (UNPROFOR's) operations in Croatia and Bosnia is that 'in war, no side would agree to give up its most important means of defence' and consequently that 'a full-scale enforced disarmament operation is only feasible as long as the security concerns of the parties are met'.[26] Even the most limited form of progress, briefly in Sector West in 1993, was only possible when a 'mutually acceptable agreement ... met with parties' interest'.[27]

It must also be stressed, however, that while disarmament under the circumstances described above can be highly destabilising, a conscious decision not to prioritise disarmament or, indeed, actually to rearm warring parties in order to establish a 'local balance of power' (as the US promised to do with the Bosnian Army following the November 1995 General Framework Agreement for Peace in Bosnia and Herzegovina, or Dayton Agreement), also carries serious risks of destabilisation unless it is clearly understood and accepted as a necessary requirement for overall political and military stability. But perhaps the most important lesson of the UN's role in the former Yugoslavia is that without an overall political strategy supporting disarmament, progress will always be susceptible to reversal.

Absence of Political Strategy
Without a coherent political strategy to underpin disarmament and weapons-control, overcoming technical and military challenges will be of little avail. The point here, however, is clearly not to adopt *any* political strategy, but to adopt a policy rooted in an appreciation and understanding of the politics, culture and history of the parties on the ground. In Somalia this fundamental failing was evident already under UNITAF. When, on 11 December 1992, Robert Oakly, chief of the US liaison office in Mogadishu, signed a cease-fire with (and openly embraced) the principal faction leaders – Ali Mahdi Mohamed of the United Somali Congress (USC) and General Mohamed Farah Aideed of the Somali National Alliance (SNA) – he not only violated UNITAF guidelines, but effectively gave the warlords a 'spurious legitimacy as political leaders'.[28] This, in turn, was a rejection of Mohamed Sahnoun's 'bottom-up strategy', and effectively limited 'the freedom of action searching for a political solution'.[29] This was also a rejection of the '"traditional" means of conflict resolution' known and practised by the Somalis themselves.[30] Again the comparison with developments in Somaliland is instructive. Here the relative success of the Conference of

National Reconciliation at Boroma in early 1993 has been persuasively attributed to the workings of 'an indigenous Somali reconciliation process ... in which the responsibilities of the function of elders as mediators in the internal affairs of the communities' proved crucial.[31]

The lack of clear political strategy became even more apparent, with catastrophic effect, during the UNOSOM II period. As the nature of the operation's goals made it essential that military operations were subordinate to and closely coordinated with the broader political process that the UN was seeking to promote, the decision to order a manhunt for Mohamed Farah Aideed not only betrayed insensitivity to the cultural context of Somalia, but also to the nature of Somali politics.[32] Even before that decision was made, Aideed had some reason to believe, as he did with ever-increasing fervour in the course of UNOSOM II, that the 'UN was bent on marginalising him politically in favour of promoting the ideas of Madhi and his allies'.[33] The killing of more than 20 Pakistani soldiers by forces *'apparently* belonging to the United Somali Congress' prompted a UN Resolution that effectively declared war on General Aideed and his allies.[34] The manhunt – which came to include a $25,000 reward and the despatch in August 1993 of US Special Forces units exclusively tasked with apprehending Aideed and his staff – was initiated by the Special Representative of the Secretary-General in Somalia, Admiral Jonathan Howe. The subsequent course of events has been examined elsewhere and will not be retold here. Its consequences, however, were clear: the UN was actively taking sides in the conflict, thus directly affecting the balance of power inside the country and among the clan-based militias.[35] UNOSOM II failed principally because the perceived need to disarm factions, and later specifically to capture Aideed, became divorced from the overall objective of the UN's involvement in Somalia.

Limited Political Will

The discussion thus far leads to the conclusion that, in the words of Abide, 'disarmament need not be initiated in a mission unless there is a will to see it through'; and if it is initiated it should be 'followed through with discipline, courage, zeal and consistency'.[36] This, however, only highlights the third factor mentioned above: the evident lack of will of outside powers to engage in coercive disarmament and commit resources to an operation where the appeal to 'national interest' is unlikely to convince a sceptical public accustomed to peacetime standards for 'acceptable' levels of casualties in operations short of war.

The limits of domestic political support for operations with a high risk of casualties is perhaps best illustrated by the case of Haiti where, in September 1994, the US administration was prepared to launch an enforcement operation, having first judged any military resistance that might be offered by the Haitian military *junta* to be negligible. After the experiences in Somalia, humanitarian arguments alone were unlikely to be sufficient to spur the Clinton administration into action. The historic role of the US in the region; human-rights violations by the *de facto* regime; the lack of effective military opposition; and domestic concerns about the influx of refugees, all seemed to suggest that using force could be justified by appealing to US interest. Still, opposition within Congress to the proposed course of action was fierce. This suggests, at the very least, that domestic political backing for coercive strategies will be even more limited where an appeal to 'interest' can less plausibly be invoked.

This question of political support, of wider relevance to the issue of external support for demobilisation, is not confined to the US. Indeed, the US decision in October 1993 to withdraw from Somalia by the end of March 1994 was followed within days by similar decisions in Australia, Belgium, Canada, France, Germany, Ireland, Italy, New Zealand, Norway, Sweden and Turkey. While many cited dependence on US logistical support as a reason for withdrawal, few accept it as the only, let alone predominant, motivation.

Alternatives to Coercion: Building Confidence and Consent
The emphasis above on the limits of coercion is not to suggest that a passive posture is the only one which an outside force can take, nor is it to rule out the use of force altogether. Indeed, as David Cox perceptively notes, there is also an area of activity in disarmament operations 'between passivity and the resort to force which may prejudice or irreparably transform the broader mission objectives'.[37] What recent experience does demonstrate, however, is that once the actions of an outside force are perceived by any of the parties to undermine their position either militarily or politically, progress will stall. In conflicts with few signs of progress on the political front, the parties' perceptions will always be more easily influenced in a negative direction. A basic sense of security and growing faith in the political processes aimed at resolving the conflict are prerequisites for progress in other spheres. It is to this end that measures that rely on the parties' consent to tackle the problem of arms are geared, however grudgingly that consent is given.

Weapons Buy-Back Programmes

One consequence of the Somali debacle and the general reluctance of UN member-states to engage in coercive disarmament has been to turn attention to consent-based schemes, especially providing incentives to defuse the threat posed by the abundance of arms. Attention has focused in particular on the efficacy of weapons-control policies and policies to reduce their circulation among the civilian population, through financial and material incentives. An important motivation behind this approach, as noted above, is that weapons usually have an economic as well as security value.

Weapons 'buy-back' or exchange schemes have been tested in Nicaragua and Panama, as well as in some US inner cities, albeit on a smaller scale. The success rate of such reclaiming schemes, however, has been decidedly mixed.

As part of the demobilisation process of the Nicaraguan resistance (Contras) in early 1990, weapons handed in were destroyed by ONUCA in the security zones it had established throughout the country. Nevertheless, numerous weapons caches remained hidden and whatever was handed in was often unserviceable. In mid-1991, the security situation in the central and northern parts of the country deteriorated sharply as demobilised Contras took up arms, apparently in reaction to broken promises over land distribution.[38] In response to the renewed fighting between the so-called 're-Contras' and 'recompas', the government initiated a weapons buy-back programme and fixed the re-purchasing price of individual weapons well above the market rate. As a result, more than three times the planned number of weapons were bought back. In a follow-up operation, 'disarmament brigades', composed of both Sandinista and former Contra members, offered more basic necessities such as food and housing, as well as cash, in exchange for weapons.[39] While some short-term benefits undoubtedly accrued from these initiatives, their medium- to long-term effects on improving security are more uncertain, not least because large numbers of weapons remain hidden. Fighting, albeit on a reduced scale, between government forces and the re-Contras continued in remote parts of the country well after the completion of the buy-back programmes.

During the early phase of *Operation Just Cause* – the US military intervention in December 1989 to oust General Manual Noriega from power in Panama – the US Army initiated a two-week weapons buy-back programme which collected nearly 9,000 weapons. As in Nicaragua, the experience suggests that a systematic and properly organised buy-back programme may have some short-term positive effects on the security environment. The specific requirements for such buy-back schemes to be effective include: creating several well-protected weapons collection points; an impartial 'no-questions-asked' policy; competitive prices, although not too much above black-market value; and the immediate destruction or secure storage of the weapons handed in.[40] Still, while the buy-back scheme in Panama produced some short-term benefits, the overall security environment clearly did not depend crucially on the outcome of the weapons buy-back programme.[41] Moreover, a number of the weapons handed in were of very poor quality, indicating that serviceable and high-quality weapons were probably kept in reserve. As shown below, this appears to be a common phenomenon in voluntary disarmament schemes where the security situation is uncertain and economic incentives for retaining weapons are greater than for selling them. In Angola, Mozambique, Central America and Cambodia, the weapons collected were also generally sub-standard.[42] Again, other confidence-building measures and, above all, evidence of progress in negotiations are essential to reduce both the security and economic value of weapons and therefore automatically increase the potential effectiveness of buy-back programmes.

Attempts to evaluate the medium- to long-term effects of pro-grammes to reclaim weapons through incentives generally confirm the above conclusions. Although experience is admittedly limited, a similar combination of factors accounts for the relatively poor record of a number of recent cases. The World Bank study of African cases noted:

> Weapons buy-back programmes have had limited medium-term impact in reducing the number of weapons circulating in countries which have: (1) porous borders with countries with active weapon markets; (2) lack of capacity to enforce regulations on the open carrying and criminal use of weapons; (3) a political, economic or security climate which enhances the security and economic value of owning and using a weapon.[43]

One or more of these conditions apply with equal force to the non-African case-studies in this paper, and clearly also influence weapons-collection attempts formally agreed by parties to a peace accord.

Incomplete Inventories and Clandestine Arms Caches
It was noted in Chapter I that even though a peace agreement may have been formally entered into by the parties to a conflict, mutual

suspicions remain strong. Consequently, parties rarely include all their weapons holdings in the inventory submitted to the monitoring force or the commission verifying the disarmament and destruction of weapons. Uncertainty surrounding the outcome of a peace process often leads to clandestine arms caches being kept in territory previously controlled by one party. While this in itself is hardly surprising, the size of the caches uncovered in Mozambique and Central America suggest that the problem is more serious than might at first have been thought.

In Mozambique, the UN accepts that weapons and ammunition have remained hidden in large quantities throughout the countryside since its departure.[44] Following complaints and investigations, the ONUMOZ Cease-fire Commission uncovered 72 arms caches containing 'undeclared war material'. Significantly, most of these were discovered during the verification process that *followed* demobilisation.[45] The process of post-demobilisation verification began in August 1994 but could not, by the UN's own admission, be completed before the ONUMOZ mandate expired in early December 1994. During that limited period 'substantial numbers of weapons were found, including tanks, anti-aircraft guns, mines, armoured personnel carriers and mortar bombs'.[46] Disturbingly, reports in late 1995 and early 1996 indicate that pockets of demobilised soldiers, especially in the provinces of Manica, Sofala and Nampula, have taken up arms and are engaged in various forms of criminal activity, while other reports speak of 'quasi assembled military units' with access to hidden arms caches still active in parts of the country.[47] Developments in Central America highlight the challenges involved even more starkly.

In May 1993, an explosion at a garage north of Managua led to the discovery of a previously undisclosed arms cache belonging to one of the 'constituent groups of the FMLN'.[48] Subsequent investigations by the United Nations Mission In El Salvador (ONUSAL), and a renewed commitment by the FMLN to disclose all arms caches, led to the discovery of another 114 secret arms caches in El Salvador, Honduras and Nicaragua. Equally worrying, and surprising at the time, was the size of the hoard and the quality of the weapons involved. Five so-called 'safe houses' in and around Managua, including the garage where the explosion had occurred, were found to contain, *inter alia*, more than 2,000kg of ammunition, 1,300 mortar grenades, 350 rockets (LAW) and 19 surface-to-air missiles.[49] ONUSAL subsequently estimated that weapons and ammunition handed in after May 1993 amounted to as much as 30% of the total FMLN stockpile. By late August 1993, ONUSAL expressed satisfaction with the process of verifying and destroying this remaining stockpile.[50] In a disturbing development in June 1995, however, the newly formed National Civilian Police in El Salvador discovered a 'major arms cache' inside the country which included 'sophisticated' weapons registered with the armed forces. The government claimed it belonged to 'armed gangs' that were linked to other groups, not only in El Salvador, but also in Nicaragua, Guatemala and Honduras.[51]

Militias, Paramilitary Groups and Weapons Circulation
Even if it were possible to disarm effectively all those who formally register in assembly areas (including those willing to exchange weapons for cash or in-kind benefits), in many cases this would only address one aspect of a much broader security problem. For example, in addition to the disarmament of regular forces in the pre-designated cantonment areas originally planned by the UN in Cambodia, more than 200,000 militia forces were also asked to hand in their personal weapons to UNTAC.[52] Moreover, as various case-studies in Africa show, 'disarming combatants at camps is insufficient in reducing the overall level of arms circulating in a country, as many combatants own more than one weapon, and many civilians are armed as well'.[53] Arming sections and certain elements of the civilian population by governments that are or have been under military pressure, has added to the challenge of weapons control. As noted above, the FRELIMO government in Mozambique is believed to have distributed more than one million AK-47 rifles to civilian 'self-defence units' in the 1980s. By contrast, ONUMOZ registered and collected a total of 213,951 weapons, a figure which, incidentally, 'exceeded by far the requirements of the new army'.[54] Similarly, one of the tasks facing a future operation in Guatemala will be to disarm and demobilise an estimated 400,000 members of the so-called Voluntary Civil Defence Committees.[55] The high number of weapons found in private hands in societies where disarmament has been attempted is also in some instances linked to the fact that the ownership and public display of weapons is culturally rooted.[56]

Conclusions: The Primacy of Politics
Clearly, disarmament and weapons-control measures have limited value unless those that are being disarmed are reasonably satisfied with the

security and economic incentives offered in return. In the short to medium term, disarmament in the strict sense is not only unrealistic, but potentially destabilising since it is unlikely ever to be uniformly and systematically implemented. Indeed, in Zimbabwe, disarming the Patriotic Front (PF) and the Rhodesian Security Forces (RSF) in 1979–80 before elections were held was deliberately excluded from the mandate of the Commonwealth Monitoring Force (CMF). This very fact, along with the consensual and 'minimalist, non-threatening posture' adopted by the CMF was, according to a study by Jeremy Ginifer, the key to success.[57]

> If the PF and RSF had given up arms they might only have heightened their own insecurities – was it really credible in the eyes of the PF that the RSF would hand in its arms or *vice versa*? The strategy of geographically distancing the parties and permitting them to retain their arms might be seen in retrospect as an inspired approach to the Rhodesia demilitarisation problem, albeit one partly forced on the British negotiators.[58]

Most fundamentally, as Ginifer also makes clear, the 'political conditions in Rhodesia, including the animosities between key leaders, and the intensity of the civil war, made any agreement virtually impossible'.[59]

Experience since 1989 confirms the primacy of political considerations and the need for a measure of trust before disarmament can effectively begin. While the attitudes of parties to disarmament are not immutable, the above discussion underscores two conclusions in particular. First, if the consequences of disarmament and weapons-control policies are not carefully considered in terms of their likely impact on the local balance of influence and power among contending factions, the overall security situation may well deteriorate rather than be enhanced. Second, if international support for operations cannot be sustained, the end result of a 'fits-and-starts' policy may be worse.

Partly for these reasons consent-based approaches to weapons control have proved, and are likely to remain, relatively more successful than those involving coercion. Even so, voluntary disarmament has its clear limitations and is unlikely to have a lasting impact unless it is accompanied by other confidence-building measures. These, in turn, must proceed, along with a political strategy, from an understanding of the society, customs and cultural context in which they are pursued.[60] Experience also strongly suggests that a *regional* approach is needed for disarmament to be effective in the long run.

There is a sense, therefore, in which the basic premise on which proponents of arms control in the 1960s and 1970s challenged advocates of 'general and complete disarmament' remains valid to the contemporary challenge of conventional weaponry after civil wars – namely, that there is 'no inherent relationship between the act of disarming and the solution to conflicts'.[61] Put differently, while the challenge of weapons is real, disarmament *per se* does not necessarily enhance security unless it is part of a broader political process that seeks to reconcile conflicting parties and enhance security by an admixture of confidence-building means. The International Body established jointly by the British and Irish governments in November 1995 to 'provide an independent assessment' of the issue of decommissioning paramilitary organisations in Northern Ireland reached, in effect, similar conclusions about the importance of confidence-building and the relationship between political progress and arms.[62] Recognising that the 'decommissioning issue' was 'a symptom of a larger problem: the absence of trust', and that an 'impasse' had been reached over the question of whether or not decommissioning should commence before all party-negotiations, the International Body suggested that the 'parties should consider an approach under which some decommissioning would take place during the process of all-party negotiations, rather than before or after as the parties now urge'.[63] This, the International Body further hoped, would give the 'parties an opportunity to use the process of decommissioning to build confidence one step at a time during negotiations. As progress is made on political issues, even modest mutual steps on decommissioning could help create the atmosphere needed for further steps in a progressive pattern of mounting trust and confidence'.[64]

III. DEMOBILISATION AND REINTEGRATION

The disarmament and weapons-control measures discussed above focus chiefly on the immediate security requirements of warring parties, civilian populations and outside agencies assisting in rehabilitation efforts. The underlying fragility of post-conflict situations, however, can only be overcome when weapons-control measures are linked to demobilisation and reintegration programmes for ex-combatants. *Demobilisation* is understood here as the formal disbanding of military formations and, at the individual level, as the process of releasing combatants from a mobilised state. It covers a number of activities associated with establishing and maintaining assembly areas.[1] These include: surveys of soldiers' needs and aspirations; medical examinations, counselling; initial reintegration packages; and transport to the community of choice.[2] *Reintegration* refers to medium- and long-term programmes, including 'cash compensation, training or income generation meant to increase the potential for economic and social reintegration of ex-combatants and their families'.[3] Although helpful for conceptual and planning purposes, the distinctions drawn between various phases and kinds of activities is to some extent artificial. Indeed, not only do demobilisation and reintegration activities overlap, but the extent to which their interdependence is recognised and incorporated into funding and implementation plans is vital for their long-term success. Particular problems are associated with the creation of new armed forces recruited from the ranks of formerly opposing armies, as well as to the distinct but related challenge of demilitarising public security and establishing credible police forces.

Long-term Rehabilitation versus Post-Conflict Stabilisation
The cessation of armed conflict, especially when formalised within a general peace agreement, is always and everywhere welcomed by war-weary civilian populations. The attitudes of military personnel about to be released from service, however, are more complex. At the same time, their attitudes are also more critical to the long-term viability of any agreement. For example, the hopes for peace in Angola in September 1992, reflected in an astonishingly high turn-out – nearly 90% – for multi-party elections, were dashed by the military commanders' decision to resume the civil war. Expectations of immediate rewards and recognition for sacrifices made during war are

often tinged with fear and uncertainty about the social and economic difficulties of adjusting to civilian life. The potentially destabilising consequences of failing to meet these expectations have been evident in parts of Africa and Central America.

A survey of demobilisation programmes in Southern Africa in the 1980s found that failure to address the needs of underpaid and demoralised ex-combatants increased the 'potential of discontented demobilised soldiers for destabilisation ... through political and criminal activities'.[4] In Mozambique, a steady stream of demobilised soldiers in search of employment have, since early 1995, moved from rural communities (where they had been transported in 1994 as part of the demobilisation package) to urban areas where there has since been a marked increase in social unrest and criminal activity.[5] Similarly, uncertainty surrounding the long-term viability of peace in Central America stems, in part, from the failure to implement reintegration programmes. Reporting on the peace process in El Salvador in November 1993, the UN Secretary-General stressed the 'urgent need to reduce tension among those ex-combatants whose justified expectations of getting land, credit and housing had been largely unfulfilled'.[6] Nearly a year later, in September 1994, former soldiers occupied the parliament building in the capital demanding that the peace agreement be implemented, while the Association of the Demobilised of the Armed Forces threatened to sabotage the economy unless redundancy payments, credit and, above all, land were issued as promised under the peace accord.[7] Delays in land distribution and reintegrating ex-combatants continue to be a potential source of major social and political unrest.[8] The consequences if such issues are not adequately addressed are clearly illustrated by the developments in Nicaragua in late 1991 where, as Baranyi and North note, the rise of the 're-Contra' resulted from the

> incapacity of President Chamorro to live up to the commitments in the Managua Protocol, that is, the provision of land and economic assistance to the demobilised force. Nor was her Government able to address adequately the social and economic repercussions of the subsequent demobilisation of more than two-thirds of the members of the *Ejercito Popular Sandinista* (EPS). They along with about 100,000 civilians also remained in possession of a large quantity of arms and some of them organised a 'self-defence movement' of 'recompas' against 'recontras'.[9]

Against such a background the international development and donor community have increasingly stressed the need for demobilisation and reintegration to be seen as part of an 'emergency to relief to development continuum'.[10] Their central argument is that disarmament, demobilisation and reintegration must be fully integrated as activities, and that short-term 'emergency' concerns should not be allowed to undermine long-term developmental goals. There is, in the abstract, an incontestable logic to this position. Yet it may be unrealistic to expect the full range of activities outlined above to be fully integrated in one operation.

The political uncertainty that invariably bedevils a continuing peace process, the various motives that lead outside powers to support an operation and, as will be argued more fully in Chapter IV, the sheer range of external actors involved (often in a largely autonomous capacity), all place very real strains on long-term policy coherence.[11] Added to this is the factor of time. In cases such as Angola, Mozambique and Rwanda, the economic and social transition from war to peace will take a full generation and should, ideally, be planned with this kind of time-span in mind.[12] However, experience since 1989 shows that once a government has disengaged from a demobilisation operation (say, by withdrawing its military, civilian and/or financial participation from a UN-sponsored field operation), it is difficult for it to sustain a commitment to long-term objectives whose effects are rarely discernible within the electoral cycle that often governs decision-making.

A further and more pertinent consideration for this study is that in the initial stages of a demobilisation process the predominant concern is usually to reduce tensions among ex-combatants in the short run. Failure to do so can easily derail the process altogether. One of the on-going discussions between the ONUMOZ leadership and various specialised agencies concerned with long-term reconstruction in Mozambique, was whether initial reintegration arrangements should simply be viewed as a 'buying-out process' or whether they should be tied more closely to a development strategy from the outset. The latter would have required greater emphasis on strengthening local institutions and capacities, but would also have been a more drawn-out process. This kind of tension stemmed, according to Aldo Ajello, from the emphasis of UN specialised agencies on a 'long-term educational approach in assembly areas', while peacekeeping staff concentrated on the 'smooth conduct of demobilisation and on keeping the assembled soldiers from taking up their arms again'.[13] As such, it was partly a clash between 'the culture of development versus necessities of peace-keeping'.[14]

The tensions between short-term 'necessities' and long-term objectives are present in all operations. Indeed, the more multifaceted and ambitious peacekeeping operations in recent years have made these tensions a central dilemma. In order to overcome as far as possible some of these tensions, and thus reduce the dangers of derailing a continuing peace process, a number of lessons have been learned from operations since 1989. These relate to the encampment and subsequent demobilisation of soldiers, as well as to the initial steps taken to reintegrate them into civilian life.

Encampment and Demobilisation

The cantonment of soldiers and the preparations made for their transition to civilian life ('civilianisation') have proved critical to the initial success of demobilisation and reintegration programmes. Indeed, according to Ajello, the two 'innovations' that had 'made the difference' by ensuring the 'successful implementation of the Peace Agreement' in Mozambique, were the creation of a Technical Unit for Demobilisation and a Reintegration Support Scheme to address the immediate needs of soldiers after their discharge from the assembly area.[15] The Reintegration Support Scheme is a reminder that, ideally, encampment should be a preparatory stage for reintegration. In reality, this is rarely the case. Operations in Mozambique and elsewhere have highlighted two basic and closely related problems which merit special attention: logistic supportability; and social and political unrest caused by delays, poor planning, inadequate management and financing of the assembly areas. Failure to address these problems invariably heightens the chances of derailment and may even contribute to the complete collapse of demobilisation operations.

The cantonment of large numbers of soldiers has required coordinated and effective logistic arrangements to provide, at the very least: transport to assembly areas; water and sanitation; food and accommodation; and the necessary measures to destroy or properly secure the weapons and ammunition handed in by soldiers. Providing such support has been fraught with technical difficulties, and has usually been impeded by the lack of infrastructure in the countries concerned, as well as by the remoteness of assembly areas from trans-port routes and sources of supply. The severely ravaged transport infrastructure in Angola (combined with the mining of all major roads), and the virtual absence of local sources of supply for UNAVEM II, account in part for the food shortages in several of the more remote cantonment areas in 1992.[16] The quartering of UNITA and government troops under the November 1994 Lusaka Protocol has also suffered from logistics deficiencies and poor coordination between the Humanitarian Assistance Coordination Unit (UCAH) and UNAVEM III.[17] In Mozambique, a Technical Unit for Demobilisation was set up by ONUMOZ to ensure that 49 assembly areas were supplied with food, water and health care while preparations were made for the soldiers' 'civilianisation' (a process that included issuing a demobilisation subsidy in two instalments, clothing and transport home).[18] Even so, supporting the assembly areas presented a major challenge throughout 1994.

In both Mozambique and Angola, the location of assembly areas and the limited logistics capability of UN forces severely complicated the tasks of re-supply. Troop assembly points, however, were often chosen by the parties themselves for strategic and political reasons and not for their proximity to supply points or transport routes. A key concern of guerrilla forces during an uncertain and fragile peace process will often be to ensure that their ability to resume, or credibly threaten to resume, fighting is not lost too early in the process. Consequently, locating assembly points in heavily mine-infested areas (often close, as it turns out later, to the guerrillas' own undeclared arms caches) is sometimes a pre-condition for cooperation. In Mozambique, the *Resistência Nacional Moçambicana* (RENAMO) insisted on establishing camps in territory which it had controlled during the war, resulting in a 'large number of sites that were unacceptable to ONUMOZ because of their inaccessibility, lack of basic security (mines) or usable infrastructure'.[19] Nevertheless, in the end ONUMOZ was obliged to supply ten assembly areas by air, adding to overall costs and further delaying the encampment period for soldiers.

Such delays, combined with the absence of educational and job-training schemes in the camps, have in turn contributed to a more serious problem: growing social and political unrest during encampment.[20] A review of demobilisation efforts in the Horn of Africa found that when ex-combatants were held in assembly areas 'without a clear perspective on improving conditions for themselves and their families, it can easily cause frustration and worse … They will feel imprisoned rather than preparing for building a livelihood for themselves and their dependants'.[21] In the self-proclaimed Republic of Somaliland, lack of resources and funding meant that soldiers were kept in camps for eight months without training opportunities or reintegration schemes; in the end, many simply left the assembly areas.[22] In Zimbabwe, former guerrilla fighters spent more than 12 months at the designated assembly points. During the ONUMOZ operation in Mozambique, delays also led to longer-than-expected periods in assembly areas. This, combined with delays in paying soldiers, poor sanitation and irregular food and water supplies, led to a sharp increase in the number of disturbances inside the camps in the first quarter of 1994.[23]

The most depressing case, however, is again Angola in 1991–92, where inadequate preparations created conditions in the assembly areas that contributed to a rapid deterioration in security both in and around the camps. In December 1991, the *New York Times* reported on 'appalling living conditions in several camps' with acute 'shortages of food, medicine and clothes', while in some government assembly areas encamped soldiers were reportedly 'close to starvation'.[24] Not surprisingly, many soldiers responded by leaving the camps; while some went hunting with individual weapons, others took up banditry.

These cases suggest that if cantonment is likely to be prolonged, provisions must be made to reduce the incentives for desertion and violence among soldiers. To minimise the potential for large-scale violence, weapons must be registered and, more importantly, weapons storage sites separated from assembly areas more effectively. In 1992 in Angola, weapons were 'stored either at the assembly area or at locations chosen by the Government and UNITA', enabling soldiers to rearm quickly once the process began to unravel.[25] In Mozambique, a partially successful attempt was made to store personal weapons in sealed containers away from the assembly area.

The difficulties described above have led troop-contributing countries, specialised agencies and NGOs directly involved in cantonment operations to emphasise the need to keep the cantonment period as short as possible. There is also a financial argument for this as the logistic demands of re-supplying assembly areas over extended periods of time are costly and difficult to finance. But more importantly, returning soldiers to their communities – as long as reintegration packages allow them to resume productive activity – contributes more directly to economic reconstruction and social integration.

'Civilianisation' and Initial Support for Ex-Combatants

In order to help ex-combatants to reintegrate it is vital to identify both the aspirations and capabilities of the demobilised population. Indeed, the success of the transition from demobilisation to reintegration is closely linked to the number of comprehensive and meaningful surveys of the population previously undertaken. The characteristics of a demobilised population vary greatly from case to case and the relative merits of incentive schemes, whether material or financial (or a combination of both), must take account of such differences. For example, Colletta and Ball identified the following characteristics of a 'typical' veteran from Uganda's National Resistance Army: male; 20–30 years old; married with 2.17 dependants; primary-school-educated, semi-literate and unskilled; with no housing; intends to live as a peasant farmer; and with a 30% chance of serious medical disability.[26] By contrast, in Eritrea, the victorious Eritrean People's Liberation Front (EPLF) contained an unusually high number of women within its ranks (more than 30% in 1991); its soldiers ranged in age from 26 to 45 and the majority of ex-fighters (an estimated 53%) expressed a preference for office work rather than agriculture.[27] In Liberia, an estimated 25% of the 50,000–60,000 to be demobilised are children, which in turn generates particular requirements.

Many of these differences stem from the fact that armed formations subject to demobilisation differ widely, ranging from disciplined, strictly hierarchical and semi-conventional forces, such as the EPLF in Eritrea, to ill-structured militia formations where distinctions between civilians and combatants are blurred (e.g., the Rwandan *interahamwe* and Somali 'morians').[28] Yet, in spite of these variations, some common characteristics are discernible and provide an overall context for considering the effectiveness of various kinds of reintegration assistance.

First, the majority of countries concerned are low-income countries where agriculture is dominant and reintegration support schemes have been initiated against a background of inadequate employment opportunities, few professional skills, limited savings and low levels of education among combatants.[29] In Mozambique, the Commission for the Reintegration of Demobilised Soldiers (CORE) noted in January 1994 that 'virtually the only option for most former combatants will be to return to small-scale agricultural production'.[30] Such skills as ex-soldiers may possess are often confined to basic soldiering, notably maintaining and using various kinds of light and small arms.

Second, in nearly all cases, public-sector institutions have been weakened by years of war and are therefore unable to carry out the full range of governmental functions required in a transition period, including providing basic social services. Moreover, in order to prosecute the war, governments have often accumulated very substantial debts, thus further weakening their ability to assist demobilised soldiers adequately, often at the most critical post-conflict stage. Added to these difficulties are the effects of large-scale emigration by professionals and the most highly skilled sections of a work-force during extended conflicts. For example, according to one estimate, by the mid-1980s some 17% of all doctors and 30% of all engineers in Sudan had left the country.[31]

Finally, as indicated above, human capital flight is compounded by the fact that the physical infrastructure of the countries concerned is usually severely damaged. The agricultural sector is particularly hard hit where guerrilla forces have been fighting the government. In many cases, food insecurity remains a challenge long after the formal cessation of hostilities. Angola, once self-sufficient in food production, now relies on food aid to feed its urban population while agricultural exports (the country once exported maize) have all but collapsed. An additional and related characteristic of countries emerging from conflict is often substantial environmental damage, typically caused by over-exploiting marginal land, large and frequent population movements, and extensive and indiscriminate mine-laying.[32]

To meet the needs of ex-combatants in such circumstances, assistance during the period between demobilisation and permanent employment is essential. This period may vary in length, although, along with the actual encampment phase with which it overlaps, it is the most critical one in terms of the underlying political fragility of the demobilisation process. Expectations among ex-combatants are usually high at this early stage, and failure to satisfy such expectations, as contemporary experience readily shows, can quickly generate social and political unrest.

Initial Reintegration Support for Demobilised Soldiers
While assistance has taken various forms, it has usually involved a combination of cash payments (lump-sum or instalments) and various forms of reintegration support to facilitate the transition to civilian life. Reintegration support has included enrolment in vocational training programmes; job-placement schemes; providing credit for small

enterprises; and allocating land and other incentives to resume agricultural activity.[33] While the distinction between demobilisation payments and reintegration assistance is often stressed for planning purposes, in practice initial cash allowances are often the primary means by which soldiers readjust to civilian life. Such cash allowances or lump-sum payments differ widely from country to country. In Angola, a $15 'resettlement allowance' was paid to ex-soldiers in 1992, whereas in Zimbabwe in 1980 the equivalent of two years' salary was offered as an incentive to voluntary demobilisation.[34] In Mozambique, the individual amount per soldier equalled six months' regular salary plus bonuses. The available record, however, shows not only that the size of cash allowances should be carefully assessed, but that 'over-reliance on cash compensation may be ineffective in reintegrating combatants and discourage them from becoming productive members of the society'.[35] Indeed, in its survey of African countries, the World Bank found that although cash payments had ranged from $50–$3,000 there was no clear correlation between the size of the sum issued and the subsequent employment rate.[36] In Zimbabwe, one of the few cases where the long-term impact of reintegration efforts can be assessed, it is generally agreed that cash allowances were too high and that they should have been more closely tied to complementary educational programmes, investment in income-generating projects, training and developing small businesses. Partly as a result of this, the number of ex-combatants either unemployed or absorbed into the public sector (including the armed forces and civil service) has been very high.[37] An authoritative study of the peace process in El Salvador also concluded that 'serious reintegration mechanisms' must 'go beyond mere cash handouts'.[38] Indeed, even if credit is specifically provided to purchase land, as envisaged in El Salvador, reintegration is not sustainable 'unless well coordinated training, technical assistance and credit for agricultural production as well as housing is provided'.[39] Finally, as Jacklyn Cock has noted regarding demobilisation in southern Africa, cash payments *per se* do not address the problems of socially integrating ex-combatants into society.[40]

Yet, while 'mere cash handouts' are clearly insufficient, cash payments have been made in part because they entail fewer logistical problems. Significantly, cash payments are often motivated by more immediate, political considerations, notably that of defusing potential unrest among ex-combatants and encouraging more rapid demobilisation. According to the International Office of Migration in Mozambique, disturbances and unrest among demobilised soldiers in Sofala, Manica and Zambesia in early 1996 only 'underscore[d] the need to complete the processing of all monetary benefits to veterans during the demobilisation period'.[41] The failure to provide 'cash handouts' was seen, in other words, as a key source of social and political unrest.

As noted above, internal discussion took place among agencies and donors supporting demobilisation in Mozambique over whether resources should be devoted first and foremost to short-term objectives aimed at reducing the potential for tension among soldiers awaiting demobilisation, or whether long-term reintegration should be emphasised.[42] Political considerations of this nature, while always present, vary depending on the context. They underscore again, however, the importance of basing operational planning on surveys of the demobilised population and a keen knowledge of local conditions and political sensitivities. Particularly important in this respect is an appreciation of the needs of different categories of personnel and war-affected groups, without whose support (even if it is only tacit) a peace process will always be vulnerable to collapse. Specifically, demobilisation operations on the scale examined in this study will always involve large numbers of senior officers who, as one ILO study rightly emphasises, 'are a particularly sensitive group in terms of power, organisational ability, management experience, resources and higher expectations'.[43] As will be argued more fully below, personnel that have been associated with the intelligence and security services present a particular challenge. Recognising such differences in background may sometimes require special treatment. In Mozambique, officers were given a larger cash allowance as it was believed, rightly, that their potential for discontent was greater, especially from middle-ranking officers. Experience since 1989 also shows that the requirements of other war-affected groups during demobilisation and reintegration need special consideration. These include: disabled veterans; female ex-combatants; dependants; and, above all, child soldiers.[44]

A delicate and difficult balance must therefore be struck between the requirements of political stability among ex-combatants and the need to design cash compensation schemes and reintegration programmes that encourage long-term productive activity. In designing such programmes, the challenge lies in striking the appropriate balance between cash allowances and other benefits that enable ex-combatants to generate their own income in civilian life, while at the same time ensuring the continuing support of groups that may otherwise destabilise the political and security environment.

Community-based Programmes and the Involvement of Veterans
Although the empirical basis on which to draw firm conclusions regarding the effectiveness of initial reintegration is still patchy, some tentative assessments can be made. The most important of these is that community-based vocational training programmes aimed at developing practical skills for self-employment, administered by ex-combatants themselves (e.g., in the form of veteran associations such as the Uganda Veterans Assistance Board) and/or NGOs, have shown the greatest promise of success both in terms of cost-effectiveness and by reducing the potential for political tensions.[45] The value of involving ex-combatants directly in planning and administering demobilisation has been demonstrated in Somaliland and Eritrea. In Somaliland, the National Demobilisation Commission (NDC), established by the government in 1993 following the Borama Peace Agreement, designed a demobilisation and reintegration programme in consultation with the veterans' association. Involving veterans and militiamen directly in planning demobilisation operations has had a positive effect on the speed with which demobilisation proceeds and the willingness of fighters to abandon other, less agreeable means of income-generation, such as banditry, looting and collection at road-blocks.[46] In Ethiopia, the most successful reintegration programmes to date have been those where NGOs coordinated their activities with the Commission for the Rehabilitation of Former Members of the Army and Disabled War Veterans, established in June 1991 to facilitate demobilisation and reintegration.[47] In mid-1995, the association of demobilised soldiers in Mozambique, ADEMO, started to work with the Working Group on Reintegration Programmes for Demobilised Soldiers 'in its efforts to provide nation-wide small-scale localised projects as opposed to the government-sponsored and centralist concept of a development brigade'.[48]

The initially promising efforts of certain donor agencies, notably the German Agency for Technical Cooperation (Gesellschaft Für Technische Zusammenarbeit – GTZ), also appear to be linked to their decentralised approach to reintegration activities. In Ethiopia, the GTZ has financed an Open Fund to support 'self-help initiatives' allowing ex-fighters to participate in small-scale housing and construction programmes and, in Mozambique, has set up a Reintegration Fund used by former combatants to finance vocational training programmes and small business development in the community.[49]

One reason for the relative success of community-based programmes, especially involving veterans, is that they are more sensitive to local needs and, on the basis of the limited evidence that does exist, appear not only to offer more flexibility, but also to be better geared towards integrating ex-combatants and their dependants into society. At the same time, the results of community-based initiatives are more easily monitored, and corrective action more easily taken, than with large-scale, centralised and state-managed programmes. These, by contrast, have proved ill-suited for short-to-medium-term reintegration efforts. In Zimbabwe in 1980, the government launched Soldiers Employed in Economic Development (*Operation Seed*) to reintegrate ex-combatants into productive life by spurring them to 'swap their guns for picks and shovels'.[50] Poor planning, ill-defined objectives and ex-combatants' suspicions about the programme's aims explain in part why, according to one close observer, *Operation Seed* 'just fizzled out'.[51] The record of achievement of the Namibian Development Brigade in the early 1990s, that has served as a focus of national reintegration efforts, has also been highly uneven.[52]

The long-term assessment of demobilisation and reintegration efforts in Zimbabwe is not encouraging. The World Bank estimates that in 1993 the government of Zimbabwe was paying salaries to 55% of ex-combatants while another 17% were unemployed. A more recent assessment has concluded that:

> The Zimbabwe experience, popularly believed to have been a successful demobilisation and reintegration of non-statutory forces but never fully verified by long-term evaluation, is now beginning to manifest long-term failures as impoverished ex-combatants demonstrate against their neglect fifteen years on ... Initial success may in part be ascribed to higher overall skill levels combined with high levels of growth in the early years of independence.[53]

The links between demobilisation on the one hand, and creating a political, security and social climate conducive to addressing issues unresolved by war on the other, have not been explored in sufficient depth. In one of the few detailed economic case studies of the relationship between demobilisation and security, Paul Collier found that in Ethiopia and Uganda 'generalised assistance [to demobilised soldiers] seems to be needed only on a modest scale, and promises beyond the competence of the government to deliver are liable to be counterproductive' and, more specifically, that 'the attempts to link demobilisation to special employment schemes appears to be ill advised'.[54] The study, which examined the potential for an increase in both 'micro' and 'macro' insecurity following demobilisation, found that in Uganda demobilisation had not thus far led to an increase in crime except in cases where those being demobilised did not have access to land. Indeed, where land has been available, demobilisation has led to a reduction in crime as the 'majority' of soldiers have 'successfully integrated into peasant agriculture or non-farm self-employment'.[55] In cases where large groups of ex-combatants either chose, or have little option but, to return to agricultural activity, land availability clearly does become a key factor for stability.

While the general findings concerning initial reintegration efforts discussed above apply to a number of cases, there are obvious problems involved in seeking to derive too many lessons from a range of different experiences. What is more certain is that expectations among soldiers and war-affected civilian populations following a cessation of hostilities are not only a function of 'promises' made, but also stem from a generalised hope that peace will bring some visible improvement to daily life. The competent management of demobilisation and the initial reintegration phase is essential if expectations are to be, at least partly, fulfilled. The final chapter will explore more fully some of the structural impediments to effective external support for the kinds of operations discussed above.

Forming New Armies and Police Forces

Where prolonged periods of conflict have not resulted in outright victory for one party, the future role of the armed forces in society, including its composition and relationship to civilian authority, is crucial to the long-term viability of formal peace accords. This also applies to cases such as South Africa and Haiti, where the transition to democracy requires the armed forces and the police to be restructured or 'professionalised'; a process that includes removing 'tainted' elements as well as broader reforms aimed at making the security forces accountable to elected bodies. The principal challenge in both sets of cases has centred on merging and, more critically, *integrating* elements formerly at war with one another, and the creation of military and police forces that are viewed as legitimate across the political spectrum and in the communities where they are deployed. Attempts to meet these challenges are under way in several countries.

Under the November 1994 Lusaka Protocol, an estimated 75,000 UNITA and 100,000 Angolan Armed Forces troops are to be demobilised, some 75,000 of which will subsequently form the new Angolan Army.[56] In post-apartheid South Africa, a major process to integrate the South African Defence Forces with those of the formerly self-governing homelands (TBVC), the military wing of the African National Congress (MK), and the Azanian People's Liberation Army (APLA) was initiated in 1994.[57] In El Salvador and Haiti, formal agreements have been reached on the need to 'professionalise' the armed forces and the police; a euphemism that involves proper screening of elements previously engaged in human-rights violations, training for new missions and separating, in law and in practice, the functions and activities of the armed forces on the one hand, and national and regional police forces on the other.

With the exception of South Africa, however, the success rate of these endeavours has been discouraging. At one extreme, the original May 1991 peace accords for Angola stipulated that a unified Angolan Army totalling some 40,000 government soldiers and UNITA troops would be established before multi-party elections were held. The failure to unify the armed forces, along with other factors, set the stage for a resumption of civil war in September and October 1992. In Mozambique and Cambodia, the very continuity of the peace process hangs in the balance as a result of the inability to integrate and restructure the 'security sector'.[58]

While activities since 1992 have highlighted a number of technical obstacles to effectively amalgamating armies, the *sine qua non* of integration lies in creating basic trust between the parties. The extent to which trust is established determines whether a *merger* translates into genuine *integration*. The alternative, as William Shawcross observed with regard to Cambodia, is that it only 'takes place on paper' while 'continued infighting, dry payrolls, and low morale undermine cohesion'.[59]

It follows from this that outside assistance, including the institutional arrangements negotiated and enshrined in peace accords, should seek to develop mechanisms and provide incentives that allow trust to be generated and whatever margin of political commitment exhibited by the parties to be enlarged. At the very least, as will be argued more fully in Chapter IV, outside assistance should provide disincentives for defection. It would be a grievous mistake, however, to assume that political will can easily be 'manufactured' from the outside, especially where the parties involved have only been prepared to forgo their war aims and agree to a compromise settlement because they have exhausted the military options. In these circumstances, commitment to an agreement is always fragile; indeed, in some cases it may not be there at all and participation in a peace process is no more than a tactical decision to buy time or rebuild military strength. There is growing evidence, for example, that in September 1992 UNITA's leader, Jonas Savimbi, was determined to reject any electoral outcome that did not bring him to power. If this was indeed the case, no amount of outside cajoling, assistance or promises of support could have prevented a return to war.

The empirical basis on which to evaluate problems associated with merging and integrating armies and police forces is still limited. Nonetheless, if a basic commitment to peace is in place, the likelihood of derailment appears closely linked to three sets of challenges:

* providing adequate training, resources and an incentive structure for members of a newly integrated army;
* the selection and ethnic composition of the new army;
* effectively separating police and military functions, while monitoring, in particular, those bodies previously associated with security and intelligence functions.

Training, Resources and Incentives
The UN-sponsored peace plan for Mozambique, approved in December 1992, envisaged creating a joint army, the *Forcas Armadas de Defesa de Moçambique* (FADM), consisting of some 30,000 soldiers made up of government and RENAMO troops. As the UN operation got under way, however, it soon became clear that very few soldiers, especially on the FRELIMO side, were interested in joining the new army. Indeed, at one stage less than 5% of government soldiers questioned in the assembly areas expressed a wish to join.[60] The original plan had, therefore, to be abandoned. Instead, it was agreed that the army would be composed of volunteers, of whom only some 11,500 had enlisted by December 1994.[61] Since then, desertions have depleted the ranks even further. While war-weariness has undoubtedly

been a major reason for the limited interest in army life in Mozambique, the resources and incentives offered to soldiers have also been a contributing factor. Indeed, poor conditions and the limited resources for those who joined the FADM in 1994 soon generated acute social and political unrest. In March 1995, soldiers of the 8th Infantry Brigade of the newly integrated army, based some 120 miles north of the capital Maputo, mutinied in protest at their salary and living conditions. The mutiny ended when the government, deeply shaken by the experience, agreed to raise salaries, although this has done little to alleviate the overall financial crisis facing the FDAM.[62] This experience highlights the potentially destabilising role of disgruntled soldiers and the importance of providing adequate resources and training for armed forces attempting to create a legitimate and distinct post-conflict identity.

The case of Mozambique also raises the important question of whether demobilisation should *follow* the integration of all armed forces, or whether those who do not wish to join the new army should be discharged before integration. The former approach allows, at least in theory, all combatants to be registered and their economic and social needs to be identified before returning either to civilian life or to a restructured army. It does, however, add greatly to financial and logistical costs, and its adoption in the case of South Africa is viewed by some as 'a crucial and very expensive mistake'.[63] Whereas the problem in Mozambique was a shortfall in personnel, in South Africa the opposite has been the case. Thus, about 35,000 will have to be discharged from a force of 125,000 after integration as part of rationalising the armed forces. Doing so without 'necessary assistance and support programmes' may 'further contribute to the already high levels of crime and violence in the country'.[64] This problem may have been much more acute if the number of guerrillas originally expected had reported for integration.

Selection and Ethnic Composition
Selecting troops and officers with diverse military backgrounds, training and experience must strike a delicate balance between the need for professional efficiency and popular legitimacy. In many cases, legitimacy requires paying particular attention to the ethnic composition of the armed forces, not least because the potential for destabilisation is particularly acute when there is an 'ethnic dimension' to political tensions among ex-combatants.[65] Moreover, as noted in

Chapter I, during prolonged periods of intra-state conflict, the mobilisation of soldiers often occurs along ethnic lines and one of the major challenges encountered in recent integration efforts has been to overcome the ethnic divisions that war has tended to reinforce. In 1980, the integration process in Zimbabwe – that is, the merger of the old Rhodesian Army, the ZANLA (the military wing of the Zimbabwe African Nationalist Union) and ZIPRA (the military wing of the Zimbabwe African People's Union) – ran into difficulties when fighting broke out between ZANLA and ZIPRA supporters. This was aggravated by the destabilisation activities of the South African forces and disgruntled white Rhodesians. The disturbances that followed the elections in March 1980, including a mutiny in March 1981, were no doubt partly attributable to the lack of proper planning for integration before the elections.[66] But, as Martin Rupiah notes, the conflict had its origin in the '1963 division of nationalists along ethnic lines'.[67] The new government nevertheless resisted the idea of forming 'tribal battalions'; in retrospect an important and, ultimately, stabilising decision.

Separating the Police and Military and Reasserting Civilian Control
During periods of protracted conflict, powerful sections within the armed forces and the 'national security establishment' have tended to find their tasks and responsibilities considerably increased. With statutory restrictions relaxed and civilian control ineffective, the intelligence and 'security forces' community has grown, often acquiring a life and identity of its own. In some cases, creating special military and police units in times of war has posed particular problems later, both in terms of reintegration into civilian life and integration within a professional national force. An example of this was the *Koevoet* in Namibia, a counter-insurgency unit more preoccupied with terrorising the civilian population than with traditional military tasks. Because of this, and especially given its personnel composition and structure, the attempt to integrate the *Koevoet* into the local police proved, in effect, impossible. According to Steven Fanning, the UNTAG police commander, difficulties persisted in monitoring 'their activities; complaints of which included allegations of intimidation, assault, attempted murder and murder'.[68] In the end, the 'problem of *Koevoet*' was only solved when the unit was disbanded.[69]

In nearly all the cases examined in this study, the 'security sector' has included various different actors whose tasks, precise responsibilities and remit have been ill-defined. The distinction between the regular armed forces and internal security forces in particular has often been blurred in law and, more seriously, in practice. Furthermore, the lack of civilian law-enforcement agencies and the failure of judicial systems to prevent acts of violence by the security forces, have too often resulted in what the Director of the ONUSAL Human Rights Division in El Salvador once pointedly described as a 'deficit operation of the justice system'.[70] In the case of Haiti where, in the words of Necker Dessables, head of the Catholic Church's Justice and Peace Commission, the 'army's *only* job [has been] to persecute its own people', the creation of a separate police force and a justice system that command public confidence is critical.[71] It is precisely for these reasons that a National Civilian Police (PNC) has replaced the discredited National Police (PN) in El Salvador, and that a new police force is gradually being set up in Haiti. The central challenge in all these cases goes well beyond that of redefining organisational structures. Ultimately, creating police forces is only part, albeit an essential part, of the broader challenge of establishing 'a legal and institutional framework for the protection of human rights'.[72]

To this end, the importance of establishing a clear and workable distinction between army and police is beyond doubt, and a number of specific proposals have been advanced with a view to ensuring that this distinction is indeed maintained. These include: retraining soldiers for conventional army operations; improving civilian control of the armed forces; and securing the loyalty of officers to democratic institutions and practices.[73] Other proposals have stressed the need to reform budgeting practices within the 'security sector', placing greater emphasis on transparency and accountability, as well as pressing for the 'civilianisation' of business and enterprises owned and run by the military.[74] The development of a professional military ethic within newly integrated forces has also been identified as an important source of long-term legitimacy.[75] Yet, these measures are only likely to go some way towards addressing the structural and historical legacies that ultimately need to be overcome.

With respect to South Africa, Robert Henderson has noted that the 'major threat throughout De Klerk's presidency was from clandestine units linked to the government's own security establishment, some as part of the security forces [notably the Directorate of Military Intelligence of the SADF] and some with only informal or contractual links', and that 'most of Third Force's operational components were products of the "security and destabilisation" *milieu* in the Southern African region over the last three decades'.[76] More worryingly, and as a direct result of this legacy, Henderson questions whether even the government of national unity can 'isolate and control continuing Third Force violence'.[77] Moreover, the professional skills and organisational attributes of the former intelligence and security forces suggest that across-the-board demobilisation or the automatic dissolution of units is not necessarily the best option, especially when employment opportunities are limited and political tensions persist. As Deputy Minister Joe Nhlanhla has pointed out with respect to the situation in South Africa, 'the wholesale demobilisation of trained personnel from the security services, including those from the intelligence, in an environment of heightened instability can lead to the proliferation of private armies and security agencies'.[78]

In both El Salvador and Haiti, the history and legacy of political violence is particularly deep-rooted and those in power have traditionally relied on parallel or shadow systems of control and repression. In much of Central America and Haiti such systems have been clandestine and informal, adding to the weakness of formal state institutions. A further consequence of this has been the profound sense of mistrust among large sections of the population about the patently false claims that law-enforcement agencies and judicial bodies are impartial and apolitical. Indeed, their principal function has often been to instil fear rather than protect the rights of citizens. The Commission of Truth for El Salvador referred to these systemic causes of violence when, in addressing the 'death squad' phenomenon, it emphasised the 'long history of violence committed by groups that are neither part of the Government nor ordinary criminals', stating further that 'violence has formed part of the exercise of official authority, directly guided by State officials'.[79]

Although progress has been made in El Salvador since 1992 and Haiti since 1994, the deep-seated nature of these problems is clear. A detailed survey by Human Rights Watch and the National Coalition for Haitian Refugees in late 1994 and early 1995 identified a number of weaknesses in the transition process, in particular the failure of screening procedures for members of an Interim Police Force. Concerns have also been expressed by human-rights groups about the re-emergence of old power structures once international involvement is scaled down or withdrawn altogether.[80] Similarly, in El Salvador there have been complaints about inadequate screening for new recruits. In several cases, ex-members of the PN implicated in death-squad assassinations have been drafted into the newly created PNC.[81] Indeed, the deliberate delays in phasing out the PN suggested, according to senior UN officials involved in the peace process throughout the 1990s, 'a lingering reluctance to see it disappear', as did the fact that the government was unwilling to provide a list of officers discharged from security bodies that would have been 'essential to verify that they are not clandestinely joining the PNC'.[82]

In countries where civil strife has been accompanied by widespread human-rights violations perpetrated by government forces, monitoring the functioning of new military and police forces is essential. For this reason the creation and workings of outside bodies, such as the UN Mission for Guatemala (MINUGUA) in September 1994, the joint UN–Organisation of American States (OAS) Civilian Mission to Haiti (MICIVIH) and the human-rights components of ONUSAL, represent significant innovations in peacekeeping practice. Their role, usually carried out in the face of government attempts to restrict mandates and obstruct their activities, is to ascertain as far as possible whether the commitments entered into are adhered to. They have provided one of the more effective forms of external assistance in recent years. In view of the deep-seated nature of the problem of reforming law-and-order institutions, especially that of overcoming ingrained resistance on the part of traditional power elites to demilitarise public-security functions, international assistance and monitoring to support the creation of national police forces should be encouraged to continue well beyond the formal termination of peacekeeping operations. This is one of the principal 'lessons' of outside involvement in Haiti and El Salvador in the 1990s.

IV. EXTERNAL SUPPORT

The preceding chapters have demonstrated the link between the dynamics of a peace process and the manner in which disarmament, demobilisation and reintegration are implemented. Since 1989, the commitment of external sponsors and the quality of the support provided have shaped, and continue to shape, the course of events on the ground in crucial ways. For example, one of the problems that continues to undermine the peace process in El Salvador, even after the formal completion of the UN mission in 1995, has been the shortage of funds to implement basic reintegration programmes. Similarly, before the resumption of all-out conflict in Liberia in April 1996, political obstacles had already been magnified by the 'paucity of resources and logistical problems' both of which became 'major challenges in demobilisation'.[1] In Mozambique, the logistics difficulties experienced by ONUMOZ, created in part by the lack of funding, both complicated and slowed down the pace of demobilisation throughout the country. Indeed, in July 1994, some four months before multi-party elections were due to be held, both government and RENAMO forces engaged in widespread rioting, in protest at the pace of demobilisation and non-payment of allowances and salaries.[2] The collapse of the Angolan peace process in late 1992 is the clearest example of how the outcome of such a process may be affected by the implementation and external support given to the original peace accord itself.

Yet, while outside financial support is essential in nearly all cases (South Africa being the possible exception), there is no automatic relationship between the level of support alone and the likelihood of a successful outcome. External actors cannot replace political commitment, nor can they generate political momentum in the absence of trust and will among the parties. They can, however, by the manner in which support is extended, discourage defection from a peace process, thus strengthening, however subtly, the degree of commitment that does exist.[3]

Peacekeeping and Monitoring Forces: The Role of the Military
A notable feature of peacekeeping activities since 1989 has been the growing number of tasks specifically related to disarmament and demobilisation. These have typically included: registering combatants; counting, transferring and storing weapons; various forms of logistic support; and demining. Forces have also tended to assume a number of

ancillary tasks at the local or community level – medical support, repairing basic infrastructure such as water supplies and bridges, and initial assistance to small-scale reintegration activities – that have helped to build local support and trust during the initial reintegration phase. Most of the operations involving a military component have been carried out under UN auspices, although the mandates in each case have varied considerably in terms of intrusiveness. The record of achievements has also varied. In 1989 in Namibia, UNTAG, after some initial tensions and difficulties, successfully monitored the demobilisation of the local military forces that had been created during the period of South African rule: the South West African Territorial Force; the so-called 'citizen forces'; and the 'commandos'. Between April and July 1990, ONUCA effectively supported the demobilisation of more than 20,000 members of the Nicaraguan resistance at various locations inside Nicaragua and Honduras. By contrast, UNTAC in 1992–93, was unable to implement the provisions of its mandate relating to the disarmament and demobilisation of some 450,000 combatants.

Military support for disarmament and demobilisation has also been extended on a regional and bilateral basis, although to a lesser degree. In Liberia, ECOMOG has been involved in a peacekeeping operation whose mandate also calls for the disarmament and demobilisation of local factions. The resumption of large-scale fighting in 1996, however, put a temporary end to the hope that some 50,000–60,000 soldiers would be demobilised as originally envisaged.[4] The experience of ECOMOG has highlighted a number of difficulties, both in terms of resources and political constraints, associated with regional action.[5]

Bilateral initiatives, albeit on a more modest scale, have proved rather more effective. In 1979–80, the UK-led CMF in Zimbabwe helped to disarm guerrillas throughout the country.[6] More recently, and drawing on its previous experience in Africa, the British Army was also involved in training Mozambican soldiers as part of the effort to create a new unified Army before the elections in October 1994. Between 9 October and 17 December 1993, 540 instructors drawn from the Mozambique Army, the *Forcas Armadas de Moçambique* (FAM), and RENAMO were trained in Nyanga in eastern Zimbabwe for the new unified Army, the FADM. Follow-up training for the new Army within Mozambique has been provided by Portugal, France and the UK. In South Africa, the British Military and Assistance Training Team (BMATT) has effectively acted as a 'referee' in the integration process by certifying that agreed procedures and standards are applied in an even-handed fashion to all parties.[7] If bilateral assistance of this kind is synchronised with the peace process as a whole, it may prove a more cost-effective way of achieving particular objectives.[8] Moreover, as Ginifer perceptively observes with respect to the UK-led CMF in Zimbabwe, 'one of the most useful aspects of unilateralism lies in the operational advantages it potentially confers'.[9] Indeed, as Ginifer points out, 'the cohesion of the British-led mission with its clear lines of authority and relative lack of inter-state bickering could be seen to contrast favourably with a number of recent peacekeeping efforts'.[10]

The question of military support nevertheless remains controversial, especially in relief and rehabilitation efforts. Humanitarian NGOs have often been particularly critical of the contribution made by military forces. In part, such criticisms are culturally determined, linked to an understandable suspicion on the part of NGOs which cherish their independence and neutrality, and pride themselves on a non-hierarchical and consensus-oriented style of decision-making. Such attitudes often manifest themselves in criticism of the military for being too 'big and rigid' and, as a result, unable to adapt rapidly and flexibly to changing conditions on the ground. In Mozambique, for example, the Special Representative of the Secretary-General felt that the 'military component was too big and to a certain extent inefficient'.[11] Yet, he also stressed the vital importance of the military in providing logistics support and transport to both government and RENAMO forces, arguing that this capacity was 'a very strong leverage for the political component vis à vis the two parties'. The role of the military, therefore, cannot be treated in isolation, and certainly in the short to medium term, military assistance – whether provided in the context of a multilateral peacekeeping force or bilaterally – can play an important role in demobilisation operations. For such a role to be both credible and effective, however, clear tasks, an awareness of local conditions on the part of troop-contributors and, not least, coordination with other actors, are all essential.

Military Tasks and Requirements
Within a consent-based framework, the military role in disarmament, demobilisation and reintegration falls into three basic categories: verification/monitoring; logistic support; and demining.

A priority throughout the entire process is weapons control and, specifically, ensuring that effective monitoring and verification safeguards are established. These should ideally encompass both passive measures (e.g., secure storage for weapons and ammunition surrendered by forces), as well as the capacity to locate and destroy arms caches, ammunition dumps and specific production facilities. This in turn requires both adequate resources and a practicable mandate. In Cambodia, Angola and Mozambique, UN forces all suffered from a lack of personnel, tactical mobility, advanced technologies and investigative powers. Much like the aforementioned problems of incomplete, uneven or partial disarmament, lack of adequate staffing for verification tasks increases the scope for manipulation and evasion by the parties. Thus, outside involvement in several African countries has shown that the 'higher rates of demobil-isation occurred in countries with the largest ratio of observer to combatant, and with multilateral monitors who had a broad mandate'.[12] In Angola, the ratio of observers to combatant was 1 to 333; in Namibia the ratio was 1 to 6. In a fragile and uncertain political environment, verification and monitoring activity must have a basic level of credibility among the parties if it is to deter defection from participation in the process. Indeed, the Chairman of the Cease-fire Commission in Mozambique, Pier Segala, has suggested that the UN 'should not assume monitoring responsibilities unless it can guarantee that an adequate number of military observers and staff is on the ground'.[13] To compensate for manpower shortages, however, much greater use can be made of available and emerging technologies than has hitherto been the case. While there is clearly no technological 'fix' to the deeper problems raised in this paper, certain technologies have shown particular promise in the verification and monitoring aspects of disarmament and demobilisation.[14] In particular, the increasing and ever-more sophisticated range of sensor systems – such as the Micropower Impulse Radar, more advanced laser-imaging systems and improved hand/air deployed sensors – can be used to detect weapon sites and illegal activities.[15]

Numbers alone, however, do not guarantee effectiveness. Logistics support provided by the military has been indispensable in demobil-isation operations, especially for establishing, resupplying and maintaining assembly areas. At the UN, the weakness of integrated planning mechanisms, antiquated procurement procedures, a semi-permanent funding crisis and a shortage of specialised units, have all helped to make logistic support the critical and most precarious link in disarmament and demobilisation operations.

The clearest example is again offered by the experience of UNAVEM II in Angola in 1991–92. The force had originally been established in late May 1991 to 'verify the functioning of the joint machinery set up by the two sides to monitor the military and police aspects of the Bicesse Accords' and observe the elections organised by the National Electoral Council.[16] Later, however, the force was tasked with counting troops and weapons in the assembly areas, and monitoring unassembled and demobilised troops, as well as those chosen for the new Angolan armed forces. Although UNAVEM II's mandate remained technically limited, the resources available to it were plainly inadequate. About 450 unarmed military and police observers were unable to ensure effective monitoring and supervision of the demobilisation process at 46 assembly areas throughout the country. UNAVEM II's role was further impaired by poor logistic planning and a lack of funding, resulting in a shortage of vehicles, air support and reliable communications.[17]

In Mozambique, the UN force numbered more than 6,000 troops and civilians, although even here the logistic deficiencies threatened to derail demobilisation activities. The difficulties had far less to do with lack of troops than with limited tactical mobility (especially air assets) to support operations and outdated procurement regulations. In late February 1994, for example, the grounding of eight Russian Mi-8 heavy-transport helicopters, after contracts had expired, threatened to derail the entire demobilisation schedule as assembly areas became overcrowded and riots and unrest began to spread. Although the UN Secretariat in New York knew about the problem for some time, procurement regulations prevented its rapid resolution. When the UN headquarters eventually hired more helicopters, these turned out to be unsuitable (i.e., too few crews per helicopter; no night-flying capability; and too limited a range and loading capacity for operations in Mozambique). Effective procurement in UN operations thus remains a major problem.[18]

The shortage of specialised units required to set up, monitor and resupply assembly areas has also generated difficulties. In order to overcome these problems, as well as to ease the planning and budgeting of operations both for the UN Secretariat in New York and for national governments, work on a Standby Forces arrangement began in 1993 with a view to obtaining 'a precise understanding of the forces and other capabilities a member state will have available at a given state of readiness'.[19] As of November 1995, 47 countries had confirmed their 'willingness to provide standby resources'. Yet only two of these (Denmark and Jordan) have formalised arrangements through memoranda of understanding.[20] More serious as far as demobilisation and reintegration are concerned, however, is the lopsided nature of the commitments that have been made. Most of the 55,000 troops committed are infantry units and shortages persist 'especially in the areas of communications, multi-role logistics, transport, health services, engineering, mine-clearing, and transport utility aircraft'.[21] It is precisely these categories that need to be filled in order to support demobilisation activities effectively.

The issue of logistics support cannot be separated from the crisis of UN financing. Although the UN's financial difficulties have long been a subject of concern, the present situation is arguably more critical than it has ever been, and short-term remedial solutions (such as borrowing from one peacekeeping account or from the regular budget to pay for a new mission) may no longer be sufficient to stave off a 'financing disaster'.[22] The financial situation is having an increasingly negative impact on operational activities. The most urgent problem for demobilisation and disarmament operations relates to the effective financing of the preliminary surveys – of logistics and of ex-combatants – and of the start-up phase, which involves deploying the initial logistic, engineering and communications elements. With the procurement system for UN operations still highly centralised, essential services are too often crippled at the outset of an operation. While these difficulties are closely related to the lack of support from member-states (notably in their failure to pay arrears) and the failure of the Advisory Committee on Administrative and Budgetary Questions (ACABQ) to delegate more financial authority to the field, structural anomalies in organising and allocating logistics support persist. Specifically, in the field the Chief Administrative Officer (CAO) and the Chief Logistics Officer (CLO) share the logistics support function – a potential source of problems since complex operations require a much higher standard of servicing and coordination than smaller, single-purpose operations.

As noted above, an aspect of demobilisation and reintegration that has not been adequately addressed is the problem of land-mines. An estimated 80–110 million mines are believed to be planted in more than 60 countries world-wide. By far the worst affected areas, which usually also include large quantities of unexploded ordinance, are all in countries where the UN has been involved in disarmament, demobilisation and reintegration. In Angola, estimates range from 9–20 million land-mines planted over a period of more than 20 years; in Mozambique, an estimated 1–2 million mines have yet to be cleared; and in Cambodia, figures range from 7–9 million.[23]

Mine detection and removal must therefore be an integral part of demobilisation and, even more so, reintegration. As the UNTAC operation and the current UN mission in Angola have shown, mine-clearing, especially of roads, around basic infrastructure facilities and agricultural land, is vital for establishing and securing access to assembly areas, as well as for economic recovery, agricultural activity and resettling refugees. It is, however, a costly, time-consuming, labour-intensive and highly dangerous activity.[24] The average cost of clearing one mine alone has been estimated at $300–$1,000, in part because mine-clearing technologies remain under-developed.[25] While mine-field breaching technologies (such as using air fuel explosives to detonate mines by shock wave over a large area) have been developed, such technologies are ill-suited to mine-clearing as part of a demobilisation and reintegration programme for environmental and other reasons.

Current techniques for mine-clearing have in fact changed remarkably little since the Second World War and, according to UN estimates, the present rate of mine-clearing world-wide is 34 times slower than the rate of mine-laying. Although some progress has been made in individual countries such as Cambodia, where the Cambodian Mine Action Centre has been successfully established and there is considerable commercial interest (and profit) in the mine-clearing business, the scale of the problem is such that the only solution seems to lie 'in finding mine clearance methods which are markedly faster and safer'.[26] A comprehensive ban on producing, transferring, stockpiling and using land-mines, as advocated by the International Committee of the Red Cross (ICRC) at a UN meeting convened in April 1996 in Geneva to examine the effectiveness of existing restrictions on the use of land-mines, would undoubtedly have improved the situation in the medium to long term.[27] Agreement, however, could not be reached and the 'compromise' solution, focusing in particular on self-destruct and other neutralisation mechanisms for mines, can only be viewed as a significant setback in international attempts to address the land-mine crisis.[28] Meanwhile, in the absence of a technological breakthrough, mine *awareness* must continue to be a high priority for NGOs and UN specialised agencies engaged in reintegration efforts, and training local demining teams will be an important task for peacekeeping forces in the future.

Planning, Management and Funding
Coordination and Funding
Two general problems add to the overall cost, and reduce the effectiveness, of demobilisation and reintegration programmes. First, there has been a general failure to plan and coordinate activities among UN agencies, donor-countries and NGOs related to both the long-term and more immediate requirements of ex-combatants. In particular, the process of demobilisation must be closely linked to the more open-ended reintegration phase, although, as seen in Chapter III, the difficulties of doing so are considerable. The problems identified by the UN Secretary-General in November 1993 regarding the reintegration programmes originally designed for FMLN ex-combatants in El Salvador apply, to greater or lesser degree, to all UN-sponsored operations since 1989:

> First, a global strategy is lacking in the formulation of pro-grammes, and this has affected their design and planning. Second, short-term training programmes did not start at the same time and were not synchronised with the dates of demobilisation ... Third, there was no overall planning and the same mistakes were repeated in the different programmes.[29]

In short, the Secretary-General concluded that there had 'not been a clear overall strategy to ensure that ex-combatants can be reintegrated into the productive life of the country'.[30] Some two years later, as the UN operation in El Salvador was coming to a formal end, key issues regarding both the reintegration of ex-combatants and the creation of the new police force remain unresolved, prompting senior UN officials close to the peace process to caution against prematurely labelling the operation a 'success story'.[31]

Similarly, one of several factors that contributed to the debacle in Angola in late 1992 was the absence during the encampment phase of a 'well-planned reintegration programme with secured financing [which] might have provided incentives for combatants to report and stay in anticipation of benefits'.[32]

The second general problem is closely related to the first and stems from the ill-coordinated and *ad hoc* approach to funding for demobilisation and reintegration activities. A key reason for this is that donor countries and NGOs usually choose to fund only specific parts of a programme. The result is inevitably a lack of coordination, poorly integrated programmes and the consequent difficulty of attracting additional funds. Apart from the purely financial constraints that govern aid policy, several factors have encouraged this state of affairs.

Most importantly, donors are often reluctant to support projects in full without evidence of the political will and ability to implement the commitments made. By making external assistance conditional on compliance with a peace accord and the speedy implementation of specific projects, however, demobilisation programmes can easily become hostage to a political process which is, almost invariably, susceptible to temporary reversal, procrastination and tactical brinkmanship by the parties involved. In El Salvador, for example, donors 'showed a clear preference for financing specific projects, mostly in infrastructure and the environment ... As a result, commitments for peace-related programmes for the reintegration of ex-combatants into productive activity (purchase of land, agricultural credit, housing, credit for small enterprises, pensions for disabled, etc.) and for the promotion of democratic institutions' have suffered.[33] In late 1993, for example, a German-financed programme to build houses for FMLN ex-combatants was begun, although it only covered one-third of the demand. Similarly, short-term reintegration programmes for demobilised soldiers of the Salvadoran armed forces provided only for 'part of the target group'.[34] Such selective targeting, inadequate funding and poor coordination may fuel tensions and resentment among ex-combatants and, much like the possible effects of partial disarmament, may destabilise the security and political situation in the country.

Donors and specialised NGOs also sometimes bring specific preferences to bear on their decisions for funding and support. These preferences may not always, however, be ideal in terms of requirements on the ground. Donors and NGOs have, for example, shown a marked reluctance to finance security-sector reform, even though this is one of the areas where resources might most profitably be spent. Donor reluctance in this area, however, is usually linked to two additional considerations.

The first is often the lack of a recognised and credible institutional counterpart with which to plan and negotiate. Guerrilla movements that emerge from a conflict often pose a special problem in this respect. In Mozambique, the UN made a conscious effort, spearheaded by the Special Representative of the Secretary-General, to provide resources for RENAMO to become a functioning political party. While this effort, and the Trust Fund created for it, was much criticised by the government, NGOs and some donors at the time, it was deemed necessary at the time for the survival of the peace process.

Second, there has been an understandable reluctance among potential donors to allocate resources to reform military and security institutions when 'public finance is not transparent'.[35] The record of corruption and misallocation of funds associated with military establishments that have already been subject to demobilisation and restructuring, only adds to this concern. Additionally, governments receiving outside assistance have themselves often resisted – either openly or by more subtle and indirect means – attempts to restructure the security sector since this would also threaten their traditional levers of power and influence in society.

The World Bank and the International Monetary Fund
In spite of these obstacles there are signs that attitudes to external aid for military and security-sector reform may be changing. A notable development since 1990 has been the growing direct support of the World Bank for demobilisation and reintegration activities; this, despite the restrictions the Bank's mandate places on lending decisions that are not made exclusively by reference to economic criteria. Increasingly, the role of international financial institutions to support security-sector reform has been accepted as legitimate on the valid grounds that 'while its roots may be political, war to peace transition holds the promise of providing additional resources for development'.[36] In Africa, where the greater proportion of military expenditure is on personnel, large-scale and orderly demobilisation may indeed lead to resources being reoriented towards more productive development activities. Indeed, the initial stimulus for World Bank involvement in parts of Africa, notably its demobilisation activities in Uganda, was in response to government requests for ways to bring military expenditure into line with other spending priorities.

While the direct support of the World Bank and the International Monetary Fund (IMF) for specific demobilisation and reintegration programmes is a novel and welcome development, the long-term success of such programmes is likely to be more critically influenced by the broader economic strategy which these same financial institutions draw up for individual countries. There is a growing recognition that the role of the World Bank and the IMF – less through their direct involvement in demobilisation activities than by virtue of their involvement in macro-economic stabilisation and structural adjustment programmes – is critically important to the outcome and long-term viability of peace processes. The broader issues raised by this relationship, however, as well as its practical implications on the ground, have not been adequately explored.

In the particular case of El Salvador, de Soto and del Castillo have persuasively demonstrated how the peace process between 1990 and 1995 was undermined by the fact that the activities of the World Bank and the IMF were not harmonised – either at the planning or implementation levels – with those of the UN. Indeed, in 1994 they warned that the 'UN and other bodies, including the IMF and the World Bank, are overseeing separate, simultaneous processes in El Salvador that could be on a collision course'.[37] Part of the problem in El Salvador has been that donors, for reasons outlined above, have been reluctant to sponsor projects *essential* to the peace process: establishing a new police force, an effective judiciary and reintegrating ex-combatants. The lack of funds has in turn obliged the financially strapped governments of President Alfredo Cristiani and, later, President Calderón Sol to rely on internal sources of finance and, by so doing, run the risk of violating the strictures of the IMF-supported stabilisation strategy which began in 1990. As a result, in 1994 the government was faced with the choice of either rigidly adhering to the requirements of economic stabilisation, or abandoning these in favour of pressing ahead with the peace accords. According to de Soto and del Castillo, the basic reason for this unfortunate state of affairs was that 'the adjustment programme and the stabilisation plan, on the one hand, and the peace process on the other, were born and reared as if they were children of different families'.[38] In other words, they see the lack of any real dialogue – 'a communications breakdown' – between the international financial institutions and the UN as being at the heart of many of the difficulties in El Salvador. Others, however, have suggested more forcefully that the development ideology of the World Bank and the IMF, with its focus on economic liberalisation through structural adjustment, may itself be ill suited to the unique circumstances of war-ridden countries.[39]

What broader lessons should be drawn from the record of World Bank and IMF involvement in recent years? Clearly, the direct involvement of the World Bank in demobilisation activities in parts of Africa and the greater willingness to support security-sector reform are encouraging.[40] Indeed, the discussion in Chapter III of the need for a root-and-branch transformation of military, police and judicial structures after civil wars suggests that the governance-related activities of the World Bank should take greater account of the need for security-sector reform. Hitherto, however, governance-related lending by the World Bank has focused solely on promoting economic and social development since, under its Articles of Agreement, all decisions must be taken strictly 'without regard to political or other non-economic influences or considerations'.[41] Accordingly, the Bank has concentrated on public-sector management (including civil-service reform); greater accountability and transparency; and providing legal frameworks for private and public business.

Yet, as the cases examined in this paper make clear, the Bank's definition of governance as 'the manner in which power is exercised in the management of a country's economic and social resources for development' must, for it to be meaningful, include an appreciation of the role of the military sector broadly conceived.[42] This is all the more important given the World Bank's own reason for its interest in governance: a 'concern for the sustainability of the programmes and projects it helps to finance'.[43] While the Bank's mandate under its Articles of Agreement appropriately and understandably limits its role to the economic and social sphere, it needs nevertheless to be appreciated that the distinction between 'political' and 'economic' dimensions is highly artificial, especially in countries emerging from protracted periods of internal conflict.[44] At the very least, these considerations suggest that when the World Bank and the IMF are involved in politically fragile countries emerging from extended periods of conflict, their activities must be closely tailored to continuing political efforts to consolidate gains made at the negotiating table and so prevent the resurgence of conflict. Thus, in addition to encouraging security-sector reform, a greater appreciation of the role and impact of economic and structural adjustment programmes in countries moving from war to peace is needed, particularly when there is a danger that 'the financial implications of peace-related programs' may be 'in conflict with the objectives of stabilisation'.[45] Recognising this fact would suggest a relaxation of the rules of financial institutions governing concessional lending when this is required by the state of a peace process.[46]

It needs to be stressed that the unimpressive record of coordination between international financial institutions and the UN in El Salvador is hardly unique. The difficulties encountered in El Salvador reflect the larger problem of initiating any kind of integrated approach given the relative autonomy of many specialised agencies, bodies and programmes within the UN. Key agencies, several of which have been closely involved in aspects of demobilisation and reintegration, remain answerable to their own governing bodies and operate their own budgets.[47] Attempts to coordinate their activities through the UN machinery, such as the twice-yearly meetings of the Administrative Committee on Coordination (ACC) headed by the UN Secretary-General, have done virtually nothing to improve performance on the ground.

Demobilisation and Development
Major demobilisation and reintegration programmes launched as part of peacekeeping operations since 1989 have all taken place within low-income countries, characterised by vulnerable external sectors, predominantly agricultural economies and high levels of donor-dependency.[48] At the same time, the social infrastructure and productive capacity of economies that have been exposed to large-scale operations have all tended to be severely eroded. Mozambique provides only the most extreme case with per capita incomes of less than $80, external aid of about 70% of gross national product and a 3.6 % negative growth rate between 1980 and 1992.

These conditions necessitate outside assistance, yet it is also against such a background that the impact of demobilisation and reintegration activities on the local economy and social fabric of society must be evaluated. It has been observed throughout this paper that there is often a very real tension between short-term pressures for action aimed at defusing political uncertainty surrounding a peace process and long-term requirements for economic reconstruction and development. Too much 'short-termism' may undermine the prospects for long-term balanced growth and reconstruction which alone can solidify a peace process. Specifically, both the UN and donor countries have given only limited attention to the potentially destabilising impact, both socially and economically, of inserting a large international presence – with civilian, military and administrative components – in fragile and vulnerable economies. As Peter Utting has observed, a major challenge for the future lies in ensuring that 'large-scale international interventions serve to reactivate processes of economic growth without seriously distorting the economy and resulting in highly skewed patterns of resource allocation'.[49]

Preliminary assessments of the impact of UNTAC's presence in Cambodia in 1992–93 have highlighted the 'distorting impact of UNTAC expenditure' on the fragile Cambodian economy, and has underlined the need for a peacekeeping mission operating in low-income countries to take account of the structure of the local economy and the likely economic and social impact of its operations.

The overall UNTAC budget has been estimated at roughly the size of the Cambodian gross domestic product for the three years 1991–93. This inevitably created a boom in expenditure, relatively high growth rates and a significant increase in the supply of goods and services. The expenditure boom generated by UNTAC, however, was not sufficiently geared towards promoting the local economy's productive and administrative capacity and had 'distortionary effects on the labour market, public administration and the price system'.[50] Instead, the growth generated by the international presence in Cambodia was 'skewed', with urban service-sector activities (serving foreign residents and organisations) the main beneficiary.[51] Moreover, since the operation was known to be temporary, the inflow of foreign capital encouraged a speculative response from the private sector, as evidenced by the growth in the construction sector, restaurants and night-clubs. Outside the urban areas, the Cambodian population, and *especially* demobilised unskilled soldiers, benefited far less from the boom in services. Indeed, one study of the operation concluded that 'the economic impact of the UNTAC operation in 1992–1993 [has] been highly distortionary and [has] not contributed significantly to the prospects for sustainable development'.[52] The UN operations in Mozambique and Central America have not had the same distortionary impact on the local economy, although nor have they been effectively harnessed to development needs.

The broader implication here is that reintegration programmes for ex-combatants should be geared, as far as possible, towards regenerating economic growth and activating indigenous resources for sustainable development. This is clearly an 'ideal' which is subject to numerous pressures and influences. At the very least, it suggests that planning for the range of activities examined in this paper must incorporate a long-term perspective.

CONCLUSION

Success in disarming and demobilising soldiers after armed conflict depends on the extent to which warring parties and individual combatants believe that their physical and economic security will not be adversely affected by relinquishing arms and abandoning what for many is not just a profession, but also a way of life. This is of particular importance when the challenge is not merely one of demobilisation, but also involves reintegrating soldiers into civil society and creating new and legitimate structures for military and police forces. Generating trust among former enemies is by definition a long-term process and the case of Angola, more than any other, highlights the dangers of ignoring this fact.

Even so, it would be dangerously misleading to assume that all of the tensions and issues that gave rise to war in the first place simply disappear with the formal cessation of hostilities and the signing of a peace agreement. Conflicts of interest, unresolved grievances and mutual suspicions continue long after the guns have fallen silent, and the commitment of officers and soldiers to a peace process must be continuously reaffirmed and certainly cannot be taken for granted. The manner in which disarmament, demobilisation and reintegration are planned and executed can play a crucial role in securing that commitment. This does not mean that increased spending and more resources will automatically, and in all cases, translate into a successful operation. Indeed, as John Stedman observed with regard to Angola, 'resources cannot in and of themselves overcome power-hungry leaders who decide to renege on their commitments to peace, but can compensate for them and provide more of a disincentive against defection'.[1]

There is, in other words, an interplay, a subtle interaction, between the dynamics of a peace process and the manner in which the disarmament, demobilisation and reintegration provisions associated with that process are organised, funded and implemented. The challenge for policy-makers at all levels is to recognise this interplay and to identify ways in which different forms of external assistance – ranging from mediation and good offices at one end to long-term development assistance at the other – can be made to serve the overall objective of consolidating a peace process. With respect to disarmament, demobilisation and reintegration, this paper has drawn a number of general conclusions and lessons. These, all closely related, may briefly be summarised as follows:

• For both technical and political reasons, coercive disarmament in the context of an internal conflict carries considerable risks and should not be embarked on unless a number of key conditions are met. Emphasis should instead be given to developing consent-based strategies aimed at reducing the economic and security value of weapons in society rather than seeking to eliminate them from the political process altogether. 'Consent-based' should not be understood here to imply that *absolute* consent is either a feasible or necessary requirement for outside involvement. It does mean, however, that the activities of any outside force should be geared towards generating local support and enlarging the margin of consent that exists at the tactical level, thus contributing to the creation of an environment in which demobilisation and reintegration can proceed smoothly.

• As far as possible, specific provisions for demobilisation, reintegration and creating new armed forces, including some of the thornier issues and detailed aspects considered in this study, should be agreed in the course of negotiations leading to a formal peace agreement. While this will no doubt often delay and complicate the process of negotiations, it may be preferable to leaving provisions vague in the hope that they will be 'sorted out' later. Experience shows that the 'sorting out' process too easily becomes politicised as parties find reasons to halt the forward momentum of the peace process. This in turn negatively affects the attitudes and patience of donors, and complicates the task of coordinating activities among a range of different actors. Time spent in negotiations may also be used to strengthen international support behind the process, while allowing parties and mediators to focus on how best to link short-term concerns, related to maintaining cease-fires and setting up assembly areas, with long-term requirements, related to reintegration and development assistance.

• All of the cases discussed in this paper show that demobilisation and reintegration programmes can be designed and managed more efficiently. This involves, above all, treating the process as a whole, avoiding disaggregate approaches to funding and carefully linking the immediate demobilisation and disarmament stage to the subsequent phase of reintegrating soldiers into society. This is not to suggest, however, that the management of operations should be tightly and centrally directed. On the contrary, the range and complexity of the activities involved in such operations, as well as their intensely political nature, require both flexibility and a measure of improvisation on the ground.

• Assistance by international organisations, NGOs and donor countries should concentrate more than has hitherto been the case on creating and rebuilding local capacities and national institutions which – once international commitment has been scaled down or withdrawn altogether – can mitigate conflicts and grievances without the risk of renewed violence. Mechanisms and institutions for addressing unresolved tensions must be widely perceived as legitimate and credible. Particular attention must be given to public-order institutions, above all, national police forces and the judiciary. At the same time, the unique difficulties of reforming these institutions require an outside commitment, if only in the form of training and monitoring, well beyond the formal end of a demobilisation and reintegration exercise.

• Much greater attention should be devoted by donors and multilateral lending institutions to restructuring and monitoring the activities of the 'security sector', particularly those elements within it that have traditionally sought to elude civilian control and have been a major source of destabilisation and human-rights violations. In this respect, military intelligence and specially recruited paramilitary forces pose particular problems, both in terms of demobilisation and reintegration. Failure to address this issue is more likely to increase the potential for destabilisation and political unrest than is failure to reintegrate all regular units.

• The difficulties of extending effective assistance have not only been a function of limited resources and poor planning. More attention must also be given to the social and economic impact of externally sponsored demobilisation programmes on fragile and vulnerable economies. Ideally, the developmental needs of the target country should be stimulated by the international support given to the process of demobilisation and reintegration. The considerations involved, however, are often delicate and complex. As a general rule, the chances of success and of reducing long-term costs and donor-dependency lie in designing programmes that promote the productive capacities of the local economy.

• The record thus far suggests that initial reintegration efforts have shown the greatest promise of success where they have been community-based and have involved veterans directly in planning and implementing programmes. This approach, as opposed to the state-managed and highly centralised policies that have also been attempted, offers more flexibility, is more easily monitored and is also better geared towards socially integrating soldiers. It is also clear that the availability of land is very often a critical factor for stability in the short to medium term since the majority of demobilised soldiers choose to resume agricultural activity, either through choice or necessity.

• The 'land-mine crisis' is indeed a crisis and international efforts to limit the production and transfer of mines need to be intensified. In the meantime, technological advances leading to improved mine-clearing techniques, additional resources and better organisation of local demining efforts, are all needed to facilitate access to arable land for ex-soldiers and thus ease their reintegration into productive life.

One final consideration concerns the broader importance of issues, events and experiences explored in this paper. Beyond the military, financial and managerial challenges involved in mounting and sustaining large-scale field operations, there is an additional and more fundamental reason for addressing the issue of arms and soldiers after extended periods of conflict. As a number of cases examined in this paper show, the question of 'what to do with the armed forces after conflict?' is often part of a wider challenge involving the reconstruction of states that in certain crucial respects can be said to have 'collapsed' or 'failed'. Such a condition is said to exist when 'the structure, authority (legitimate power), law, and political order have fallen apart and must be reconstituted in some form, old or new'.[2] While instances of state collapse may be more or less total, the role and place in society of armed forces remains central to any process of 'state reconstitution'.[3] Indeed, even in those cases where a political order remains in place or a new one has emerged at the end of a conflict as in Eritrea, Ethiopia and Uganda, the status of the armed forces and ex-combatants in society needs to be addressed. Failure to do so, as experience since 1989 amply demonstrates, is certain to have destabilising consequences both domestically and for regions as a whole.

NOTES

Introduction

[1] Quoted in Heribert Weiland and Matthew Braham (eds), *The Namibian Peace Process: Implications and Lessons for the Future* (Freiburg: Arnold Bergsträsser Institut, 1994), p. 158.

[2] *Ibid.*

[3] For the most comprehensive comparative study of contemporary demobilisation and reintegration, see 'Demobilisation and Reintegration of Military Personnel in Africa: The Evidence from Seven Country Studies', *World Bank Discussion Paper*, no. 130, the World Bank, Washington DC, 1993 (henceforth, 'Demobilisation and Reintegration in Africa'). This has since been followed up by a further study, 'Case-Studies in War-to-Peace Transition: The Demobilisation and Reintegration of Ex-Combatants in Ethiopia, Namibia and Uganda', *World Bank Discussion Paper*, no. 331, the World Bank, Washington DC, 1996.

[4] João Paulo Borges Coelho and Alex Vines, 'Demobilisation and Reintegration of Ex-Combatants in Mozambique', Refugee Studies Programme, Queen Elizabeth House, University of Oxford, 1995, p. i.

[5] See Ramesh Srivastava, 'Framework of Guidelines for the Reintegration of Demobilised Combatants through Training and Employment' (draft), International Labour Organisation (ILO), Geneva, 1995.

[6] On the role of the development community and long-term 'peacebuilding' activities, see Nicole Ball with Tammy Halevy, 'Making Peace Work: The Role of the International Development Community', Overseas Development Council (ODC), Policy Essay 18, Washington DC, 1996. See also Patricia Weiss-Fagan, 'After Conflict: A Review of Selected Sources on Rebuilding War-torn Societies', United Nations Research Institute for Social Development (UNRISD), Geneva, 1995.

Chapter I

[1] Adam Roberts, 'Ethnic Conflict: Threat and Challenge to the UN', in Anthony McDermott (ed.), *Ethnic Conflict and International Security* (Oslo: Norwegian Institute of International Affairs, June 1994), p. 21.

[2] Stephen Baranyi, 'The Challenge in Guatemala: Verifying Human Rights, Strengthening National Institutions and Enhancing an Integrated UN Approach to Peace', Research Paper 1, Centre for the Study of Global Governance, London School of Economics and Political Science (LSE), 1995, p. 2.

[3] Kees Kingma and Vanessa Sayers, 'Demobilisation in the Horn of Africa, Proceedings of the International Resource Group (IRG) on Disarmament and Security in the Horn of Africa Workshop, Addis Ababa, 4–7 December 1994', Bonn International Center for Conversion (BICC), June 1995, p. 16.

[4] 'Donor Response to Demobilisation and Reintegration in the Horn of Africa', IRG and BICC Seminar Report, Copenhagen, 11 September 1995, p. 2.

[5] Robin Luckham, 'The Military, Militarization and Democratization in Africa: A Survey of Literature and Issues', *African Studies Review*, vol. 37, no. 2, September 1994, p. 19.

[6] These draw on Samuel Huntington, 'Civil Violence and the Process of Development', in *Civil Violence and the International System*, Adelphi Paper 83 (London: IISS, 1971), p. 12.

[7] For a fuller discussion, see Ted R. Gurr, 'Peoples Against States: Ethnopolitical Conflict and the Changing World System', *International Studies Quarterly*, vol. 38, no. 3, September 1994, which also provides useful data on the contemporary incidence of 'ethnopolitical wars' and 'communal rivalries'. On the meaning and definition of ethnonationalism, see Walker Connor, 'A Nation Is a Nation, Is a State, Is an Ethnic Group, Is a ...', in Connor, *Ethnonationalism: The Quest for Understanding* (Princeton, NJ: Princeton University Press, 1994), pp. 90–117. For an anthropological discussion of the terms 'ethnic group' and 'ethnicity', see Malcolm Chapman, Maryon McDonald and Elisabeth Tonkin, 'Introduction', in *History and Ethnicity*, ASA Monograph 27 (London: Routledge, 1989).
[8] Adam Roberts, 'Communal Conflict as a Challenge to International Organisation: The Case of Former Yugoslavia', *Review of International Studies*, vol. 21, no. 4, October 1995, p. 391.
[9] Donald Rothchild and Caroline Hartzell, 'Interstate and Intrastate Negotiations in Angola', in William Zartman (ed.), *Elusive Peace: Negotiating an End to Civil Wars* (Washington DC: Brookings, 1995), p. 175.
[10] Ioan M. Lewis, 'Making History in Somalia: Humanitarian Intervention in a Stateless Society', Centre for the Study of Global Governance, LSE, September 1993.
[11] John Markakis, 'Ethnic Conflict and the State in the Horn of Africa', in Markakis and Katsuyoshi Fukui (eds), *Ethnicity and Conflict in the Horn of Africa* (Athens, OH: Ohio University Press, 1994), p. 236.
[12] *Ibid.*, p.13.
[13] See 'Report of the Commission on the Truth for El Salvador', Annex to S/25500, 1 April 1993. For continued army involvement into the 1990s when the peace process was supposedly taking root, see 'Report of Joint Group for the Investigation of Politically Motivated Illegal Armed Groups in El Salvador', Annex to S/1994/989, 22 October 1994.
[14] Tom Lodge, 'The Post-Apartheid Army: Political Considerations', Paper Presented to a Conference organised by the Institute for Defence Policy, Pretoria, November 1993.
[15] David Keen, 'Organised Chaos: Not the New World Order We Ordered', *The World Today*, vol. 52, no.1, January 1996, and Keen, 'The Economics of War: Some Thoughts on the War Literature and the Potential Role of Economic Analysis' (draft).
[16] Mark Chingono, 'War, Economic Change and Development: The Grass-Roots War-Economy of Manica Province, 1988–92' (draft), Queen Elizabeth House, University of Oxford, 1995, p. 74. For a comprehensive study of Mozambique, see Chingono, *The State, Violence and Development: The Political Economy of War in Mozambique, 1975–92* (Aldershot: Avebury, 1996).
[17] *Ibid.*, pp. 73–74.
[18] 'Land Conflict Looms in El Salvador', *International Peacekeeping News*, vol. 1, no. 12, October 1995, p. 19.
[19] Summary of World Broadcasts (SWB), AL/2393 L/7, 28 August 1995, and 'Guatemalans Negotiating Future Role of Military', *New York Times*, 27 August 1995.
[20] 'Crackdown on Military Crime', *Latin America Monitor*, vol. 11, no. 8, August 1994, p. 9.
[21] Alvaro de Soto and Graciana del

Castillo, 'Implementation of Comprehensive Peace Agreements: Staying the Course in El Salvador', *Global Governance*, vol. 1, no. 2, May–August 1995, pp. 195–96.

[22] Alex de Waal, 'Contemporary Warfare in Africa', in Mary Kaldor (ed.), *Restructuring the Global Military Sector* (Oxford: Oxford University Press, forthcoming, 1996). See also 'Troops take Liberties in Freetown', *The Guardian*, 4 March 1995.

[23] 'Donor Response to Demobilisation and Reintegration in the Horn of Africa', p. 3. The groups are known as 'morians'.

[24] Guy Goodwin-Gill and Ilene Cohn, *Child Soldiers: The Role of Children in Armed Conflicts* (Oxford: Clarendon Press, 1994), p. 82.

[25] David Keen, 'When War Itself is Privatised', *Times Literary Supplement*, 29 December 1995, p. 13.

[26] See Swadesh Rana, *Small Arms and Intra-State Conflicts*, Research Paper 34 (Geneva: UNIDIR, 1995). For the number of conflicts in progress in 1993, see Ylva Norlander (ed.), *States in Armed Conflicts*, Report 38 (Uppsala: Department of Peace and Conflict Research, Uppsala University, 1994).

[27] See Aaron Karp, 'The Arms Trade Revolution: The Major Impact of Small Arms', *The Washington Quarterly*, vol. 17, no. 4, Autumn 1994, especially pp. 70–73.

[28] S/23613, 19 February 1992.

[29] Rana, *Small Arms and Intra-State Conflicts*, p. 6.

[30] *Ibid.*, p. 4.

[31] 'Landmines', *Africa Research Bulletin*, vol. 31, no. 1, 1994, pp. 11,587–88.

[32] For a comprehensive account of the land-mine crisis, see 'Assistance in Mine Clearance', Report of the Secretary-General, A/49/35, UN, New York, 6 September 1994.

[33] Edward J. Laurance, 'Surplus Light Weapons as a Conversion Problem: Unique Characteristics and Solutions', in Laurance and Herbert Wulf (eds), *Coping With Surplus Weapons: A Priority for Conversion Research and Policy*, Brief 3, BICC, June 1995, p. 31.

[34] Michael T. Klare, 'The Global Trade in Light Weapons and the International System in the Post-Cold War Era', in Jeffrey Boutwell, Michael T. Klare and Laura W. Reed (eds), *Lethal Commerce: The Global Trade in Small Arms and Light Weapons* (Cambridge, MA: American Academy of Arts and Sciences, 1995), p. 36. See also Ksenia Gonchar and Peter Lock, 'Small Arms and Light Weapons: Russia and the Former Soviet Union', in *ibid.*, pp. 116–23.

[35] Bruce Clark, *An Empire's New Clothes: The End of Russia's Liberal Dream* (London: Vintage, 1995), pp. 69–70.

[36] Laurance, 'Surplus Light Weapons', p. 31.

[37] On the background and consequences of light-weapon proliferation during the Afghan war, see Chris Smith, *The Diffusion of Small Arms and Light Weapons in Pakistan and Northern India* (London: Brassey's for the Centre for Defence Studies, 1993).

[38] Rana, *Small Arms and Intra-State Conflicts*, p. 6.

[39] The sources of supply are usually extremely diverse. On southern Africa, see Jacklyn Cock, 'A Sociological Account of Light Weapons Proliferation in Southern Africa', in Jasjit Singh (ed.), *Light Arms and International Security* (New Dehli: Indian Pugwash and British American Security Information Council, 1995),

pp. 98–113.
[40] David Cox, 'Peacekeeping and Disarmament: Peace Agreements, Security Council Mandates and Local Disarmament', in Virginia Gamba and Jakkie Potgieter (eds), *Managing Arms in Peace Processes: The Issues* (draft) (Geneva: UNIDIR, forthcoming, 1996), p. 83.
[41] S/1994/760, 24 June 1994, para. 20. After three months, a total of 3,192 combatants had been demobilised.
[42] Cox, 'Peacekeeping and Disarmament', p. 58 (emphasis added).
[43] de Soto and del Castillo, 'Implementation of Comprehensive Peace Agreements', pp. 195–96.
[44] *Ibid.*, p. 195.
[45] Margaret Joan Anstee, 'Angola: The Forgotten Tragedy, A Test Case for UN Peacekeeping', *International Relations*, vol. 11, no. 6, December 1994.
[46] Winrich Kühne, Bernard Weimer and Sabine Fandrych (eds), *International Workshop on the Successful Conclusion of the United Nations Operations in Mozambique*, KB 2917 (Ebenhausen: Stiftung Wissenschaft und Politik, July 1995), p. 12.
[47] *Ibid.*
[48] Quoted in Stephen J. Stedman, 'UN Intervention in Civil Wars: Imperatives of Choice and Strategy', Paper presented at the Conference 'Beyond Traditional Peacekeeping', Naval War College, Newport, RI, 23–24 February 1994, p. 13.

Chapter II
[1] For the broader context of the Somalia operation, see especially Samuel Makinda, *Seeking Peace from Chaos: Humanitarian Intervention in Somalia* (London: Lynne Rienner for the International Peace Academy, 1993), and James Mayall and Ioan M. Lewis, 'Somalia', in Mayall (ed.), *The New Interventionism* (Cambridge: Cambridge University Press, 1996).
[2] See 'The UN and the Situation in Somalia', UN Department of Public Information, New York, 1 May 1994, p. 9.
[3] See Barbara Ekwall-Uebelhart and Andrei Raevsky, *Managing Arms in Peace Processes: Croatia and Bosnia-Herzegovina* (Geneva: UNIDIR, 1996).
[4] See Jane Boulden, 'Rules of Engagement and Force Structure and Composition in UN Disarmament Operations', and Fred Tanner, 'Consensual versus Coercive Disarmament', both in Gamba and Potgieter (eds), *Managing Arms in Peace Processes: The Issues* (draft).
[5] UNSCR 794, 3 December 1992, para. 10.
[6] S/24868, 30 November 1992, p. 1.
[7] *Ibid.*, pp. 4–5.
[8] Interviews with UN HQ and UNOSOM II staff, 1994.
[9] See Kenneth Allard, *Somalia Operations: Lessons Learned* (Washington DC: National Defense University, 1995), pp. 16–18 and 36–37.
[10] See 'Somalia Lessons Learned: Light Cavalry (Coordinating Draft)', Directorate of Combat Development Analysis Division, US Army Armor Center, September 1993, p. 23.
[11] S/25354, 3 March 1993.
[12] *Ibid.*, paras 58 and 101.
[13] UNSCR 814, 26 March 1993 (emphasis added).
[14] 'Report of the Commission of Inquiry Established Pursuant to SC Resolution 885 (1993) to Investigate Armed Attacks on UNOSOM II Personnel Which Led to Casualties Among Them' (henceforth 'UNOSOM II Commission of Inquiry'), attached to S/1994/653, 1 June 1994, paras 44 and 45.
[15] Report by the Secretary-General, S/

25354, 3 March 1993, para. 91.
[16] 'UNOSOM II Commission of Inquiry', para. 52.
[17] S/24868, 30 November 1992, pp. 1–2 (emphasis added).
[18] See the eloquent and persuasive case made by Robert G. Patman, 'The UN Operations in Somalia', in Ramesh Thakur and Carlyle Thayer (eds), *A Crisis of Expectations: UN Peacekeeping in the 1990s* (Boulder, CO: Westview Press, 1995).
[19] Ioan M. Lewis, 'The Uncentralised Somali Legacy', Introduction to *A Study of Decentralised Political Structures for Somalia: a Menu of Options*, LSE, August 1995, p. xvi.
[20] Rana, *Small Arms and Intra-State Conflicts*, p. 6.
[21] Clement Adibe, *Managing Arms in Peace Processes: Somalia* (Geneva: UNIDIR, 1995), p. 104.
[22] Mohamed Sahnoun, 'Prevention in Conflict Resolution: The Case of Somalia', *Irish Studies in International Affairs*, vol. 5, 1994, p. 12.
[23] John Drysdale, 'Somali Views of Foreign Military Intervention', Paper Presented to the Conference, 'Learning from *Operation Restore Hope*: Somalia Revisited', Princeton University, NJ, 21–22 April 1995.
[24] John Mackinlay and Abiodun Alao, 'Liberia 1994: ECOMOG and UNOMIL Response to a Complex Emergency', Occasional Paper, United Nations University, Tokyo, 1995, p. 49.
[25] *Ibid.*
[26] Ekwall-Uebelhart and Raevsky, *Managing Arms in Peace Processes: Croatia and Bosnia-Herzegovina*, p. 152.
[27] *Ibid.*, p. 153.
[28] Patman, 'The UN Operations in Somalia', p. 94. See also Mark Bradbury, 'The Somali Conflict: Prospects for Peace', Oxfam Research Paper 9, *Report for OXFAM* (UK and Ireland), October 1993, pp. 101–2.
[29] Patman, 'The UN Operations in Somalia', p. 94.
[30] Bradbury, 'The Somali Conflict', p. 101; Sahnoun, 'Prevention in Conflict Resolution', p. 10.
[31] *Ibid.*, p. 74. The same holds true for the Sannag Grand Peace and Reconciliation Conferences between the Issaq and Darod clans held in the latter half of 1993. See Bradbury, 'The Somali Conflict', pp. 65–99.
[32] On UNSCR 837, the Commission of Inquiry simply observed: 'Without investigation, blame for the attacks of 5 June was laid on the USC/SNA'. See, 'UNOSOM II Commission of Inquiry', para. 125. This is certainly not to suggest that Aideed had nothing to do with the attack, nor that his role during this period did not seriously disrupt efforts to move the peace process forward.
[33] Drysdale, 'Somali Views of Foreign Military Intervention', p. 17.
[34] UNSCR 837 (emphasis added).
[35] See Drysdale, 'Somali Views of Foreign Military Intervention'.
[36] Adibe, *Managing Arms in Peace Processes: Somalia*, p. 104.
[37] Cox, 'Peacekeeping and Disarmament', p. 74
[38] 'Contra Guerrillas Take up their Arms Again', *The Independent*, 25 June 1991.
[39] 'Demobilisation and Reintegration in Africa', p. 32.
[40] *Ibid.*, p. 33
[41] Interview with senior US army personnel involved in *Operation Just Cause*. See also *ibid.*.
[42] Interviews at troop and weapons assembly areas in northern Mozambique, February 1994. See also Chris Alden, 'Swords Into Ploughshares? The United Nations and Demilitarisation in Mozambique', *International*

Peacekeeping, vol. 2, no. 2, Summer 1995, p. 188.
[43] 'Demobilisation and Reintegration in Africa', para. 173.
[44] 'Final Report of the Secretary-General on the UN Operation in Mozambique', S/1994/1449, 23 December 1994, paras 15 and 36.
[45] Comments by Pier Segala, former Chairman of the Cease-fire Commission, in Kühne, Weimer and Fandrych (eds), *International Workshop on the Successful Conclusion of the United Nations Operations in Mozambique*, p. 12.
[46] 'Final Report of the Secretary General on the UN Operation in Mozambique', para. 12.
[47] 'Incidents of Insecurity with Suspected Involvement of DS', International Organisation for Migration (Mozambique Mission), Bi-monthly Highlights, September–October 1992.
[48] 'Letter from Secretary-General to President of Security Council concerning the discovery of an FMLN weapons cache', S/25901, 8 June 1993.
[49] 'Report of the Secretary-General concerning illegal arms deposits belonging to the FMLN', S/26005, 29 June 1993.
[50] 'Report of the Secretary-General concerning the identification and destruction of clandestine arms deposits belonging to the FMLN', S/26371, 30 August 1993.
[51] 'PNC Scores Success in Crime Fight', *Latin America Monitor*, vol. 12, no. 8, August 1995, p. 9.
[52] Cox, 'Peacekeeping and Disarmament', p. 67. According to Cox, it is still 'not clear how many of the militia actually handed in their weapons'.
[53] 'Demobilisation and Reintegration in Africa', para. 172.
[54] Kühne, Weimer and Fandrych (eds), *International Workshop on the*

Successful Conclusion of the United Nations Operations in Mozambique, p. 21.
[55] Baranyi, 'The Challenge in Guatemala', p. 24.
[56] 'Demobilisation and Reintegration Issues in the Horn of Africa', in Jakkie Cilliers (ed.), *Dismissed* (Pretoria: Institute of Defence Studies, 1995).
[57] Jeremy Ginifer, *Managing Arms in Peace Processes: Rhodesia/Zimbabwe* (Geneva: UNIDIR, 1995), p. 55.
[58] *Ibid.*, p. 52.
[59] *Ibid.*, p. 51.
[60] On the failure to do so in Somalia, see Ioan M. Lewis, 'Misunderstanding Somalia', *Anthropology Today,* vol. 9, no. 4, August 1993.
[61] Philip Windsor, 'GCD Again?', *Millennium*, vol. 1, no. 1, Summer 1971, p. 68.
[62] Sen. George J. Mitchell, Gen. John de Chastelain and Harri Holkeri, *Report of the International Body (Mitchell Report)*, 22 January 1996, para. 14.
[63] *Ibid.*, para. 34.
[64] *Ibid.*, para. 35.

Chapter III
[1] While the focus here is on the assembly process, not all soldiers go through a formal encampment phase. 'Self demobilisation', that is, soldiers returning to their communities more or less un-aided after the cessation of conflict, often occurs alongside formal processes.
[2] 'Third Progress Report of the Secretary-General on the UN Observer Mission in Liberia', S/1994/463, 18 April 1994, para. 26.
[3] 'Demobilisation and Reintegration in Africa', p. vi. For a survey of some of the key challenges involved, see Ramesh Srivastava, 'Reintegrating Demobilised Combatants: A Report

Exploring Options for Training-Related Interventions', Vocational Training Systems Management Branch, ILO, Geneva, 1994.

[4] Jacklyn Cock, 'The Social Integration of Demobilised Soldiers in Contemporary Africa', *South African Defence Review*, no. 12, 1993, p. 1.

[5] Interview with senior UNHCR official for Mozambique, November 1995. According to the police, the crime rate in Mozambique increased by 10% in 1995. See 'Mozambique: A Cloudy Dawn', *Africa Confidential*, vol. 37, no. 3, 2 February 1996.

[6] S/26790, 23 November 1993, para. 51.

[7] See 'Criticism Marks First 100 Days', *Latin America Monitor*, vol. 11, no. 10, October 1994, p. 10, and 'Has the UN Withdrawn Too Soon?', *ibid.*, vol. 12, no. 6, June 1995, p. 10.

[8] Interviews at the UN, New York, April 1996.

[9] Stephen Baranyi and Liisa North, *Stretching the Limits of the Possible: United Nations Peacekeeping in Central America* (Ottawa: Canadian Centre for Global Security, 1992), pp. 15–16. See also 'Contra Fighters Wait for their Promised Land', *The Independent*, 13 March 1991.

[10] 'Donor Response to Demobilisation and Reintegration in the Horn of Africa'. See also Matthias Stieffel, 'UNDP in Conflicts and Disasters', War-torn Society Project, UNRIST, Geneva, August 1994.

[11] See 'Development Aid for Militia Reform: A Pathway to Peace', *Policy Focus*, No. 6, ODC, Washington DC, 1993.

[12] 'The Role of International Institutions in Post-Conflict Rebuilding', ODC Roundtable, Washington DC, 28 February 1996, p. 3.

[13] See Kühne, Weimer and Fandrych (eds), *International Workshop on the Successful Conclusion of the United Nations Operations in Mozambique*, pp. 13 and 25–28.

[14] *Ibid.* Interviews with ONUMOZ staff, Maputo, February 1994.

[15] *Ibid.*, p. 12.

[16] See reports by the Secretary-General on the UNAVEM II operation, S/23191, 31 October 1991, paras 20–21, and S/24145, 24 June 1992, para. 35.

[17] However, the principal source of delay in 1995 and 1996 was UNITA's unwillingness to demobilise its troops. See *Africa Confidential*, vol. 37, no. 8, 12 April 1996, and private interviews with UN senior officials, April 1996.

[18] 'Demobilisation and Assembly Areas', ONUMOZ Technical Unit for Demobilisation, Briefing Note, February 1994.

[19] *Ibid.*, and interviews with ONUMOZ personnel, February 1994.

[20] 'Demobilisation and Reintegration of Former Soldiers', Summary of Meeting (Draft), Refugee Policy Group, Washington DC, 7 June 1994.

[21] Kingma and Sayers, 'Demobilisation in the Horn of Africa', p. 16.

[22] *Ibid.*

[23] Private interviews at Namialo and Quinga camps in Nampula province, February 1994. See also Coelho and Vines, 'Demobilisation and Reintegration of Ex-Combatants in Mozambique', pp. 16–20.

[24] Quoted in 'Demobilisation and Reintegration in Africa', p. 24.

[25] 'Further Report of the Secretary-General on the United Nations Angola Verification Mission (UNAVEM II)', S/24556, 90 September 1992, para. 15.

[26] Nat Colletta and Nicole Ball, 'War to Peace Transition in Uganda', *Finance and Development*, June 1993, p. 36.

[27] Roland Marchal, 'Démobilisation et reconstruction en Érythrée', Conference Paper Presented at Centre d'Etudes Africaines, Paris, February 1995, and Kingma and Sayers, 'Demobilisation in the Horn of Africa', pp. 15–20.

[28] See de Waal, 'Contemporary Warfare in Africa'.

[29] Again there are exceptions. See Ball with Halevy, 'Making Peace Work', pp. 18–26.

[30] See 'Reintegration Support Scheme for Demobilised Soldiers', Annex 3/ CORE 5, Maputo, January 1994.

[31] An estimated 500,000 'highly trained' Sudanese were living abroad in 1985. See 'Military Conversion for Social Development', Report No. 5, BICC, July 1995, p. 15.

[32] Ball with Halevy, 'Making Peace Work', pp. 22–23.

[33] See Srivastava, 'Framework of Guidelines for the Reintegration of Demobilised Combatants', pp. 3–4. See also 'Demobilisation and Reintegration in Africa', Chapter 5.

[34] Cock, 'The Social Integration of Demobilised Soldiers', p. 13. In Zimbabwe, this amounted to $259 per month for two years. See 'Demobilisation and Reintegration in Africa', p. 63.

[35] Ibid., p. 97.

[36] Annex 1 to 'Informal Summary of World Bank Seminar on Demobilisation and Reintegration Programs of Military Personnel', 21 June 1994, p. 3.

[37] For a highly critical view of the reintegration process in Zimbabwe, see Mchaparara Musemwa, 'The Ambiguities of Democracy: The Demobilisation of the Zimbabwean Ex-Combatants and the Ordeal of Rehabilitation, 1980–1993', in Cilliers (ed.) Dismissed. Musemwa, while highly critical of government programmes, does not believe that the cash allowance was too high. For the opposite view, see 'Demobilisation and Reintegration in Africa', p. 63.

[38] Graciana del Castillo, 'Arms-for-Land Deal: Lessons form El Salvador', in Michael Doyle and Ian Johnstone (eds), Multidimensional Peacekeeping: Lessons from Cambodia and El Salvador (Cambridge: Cambridge University Press, forthcoming, 1996), p. 24.

[39] Ibid., p. 32.

[40] Cock, 'A Sociological Account', pp. 103–4.

[41] International Organisation for Migration (Mozambique Mission), Bi-monthly Highlights, January–February 1996 (draft).

[42] Coelho and Vines, 'Demobilisation and Re-integration of Ex-Combatants in Mozambique', p. 10.

[43] Ramesh Srivastava, Reintegrating Demobilised Combatants: A Report Exploring Options and Strategies for Training-related Interventions (Geneva: ILO, 1995), p. 12.

[44] On the reintegration of child soldiers, see Margaret McCalin, The Reintegration of Young Ex-Combatants into Civilian Life: A Report to the International Labour Office (Geneva: ILO, 1995).

[45] For the role of the veteran association in Uganda, see Emilio Mondo, 'Uganda's Experience in National Management of Demobilisation and Reintegration', in Cilliers (ed.), Dismissed, pp. 90–103.

[46] de Waal, 'Contemporary Warfare in Africa', p. 54.

[47] See comments by Ato Mulugeta Gebre-Hiwot, in 'Donor Response to Demobilisation and Reintegration in the Horn of Africa', p. 3.

[48] Michael F. Stephen, 'Demobilisation in Mozambique', in Cilliers (ed.), Dismissed, p. 62.

[49] 'Proposal for the Reintegration of Refugees, Displaced Persons, and Ex-Combatants with Special Reference to Sub-Saharan Africa', GTZ, Bonn, unpublished, August 1992, and private interviews.
[50] Musemwa, 'The Ambiguities of Democracy', p. 45.
[51] *Ibid.*, p. 44. For a less partisan assessment, see Martin Rupiah, 'Demobilisation and Integration: "Operation Merger" and the Zimbabwe National Defence Forces, 1980–1987', *African Security Review*, vol. 4, no. 3, 1995.
[52] Simon Shikangalah, 'The Development Brigade: The Namibian Experience', in Cilliers (ed.), *Dismissed*, pp. 70–71.
[53] Michael F. Stephen, 'Demobilisation in Mozambique', in *ibid.*, p. 68, footnote 39.
[54] Paul Collier, 'Demobilisation and Insecurity: A Study in the Economics of the Transition from War to Peace', *Journal of International Development*, vol. 6, no. 3, 1994, p. 350. See also Collier, 'Some Economic Consequences of Peace with Applications to Uganda and Ethiopia', Centre for the Study of African Economics, University of Oxford, April 1993.
[55] Collier, 'Demobilisation and Insecurity', p. 349.
[56] For the demobilisation concept adopted in the Lusaka Protocol, see Annex to 'Letter from Permanent Representative of Angola to President of the Security Council', S/1994/1441, 22 December 1994.
[57] On the integration process in South Africa, see Tsepe Motumi and Andrew Hudson, 'Rightsizing: The Challenges of Demobilisation and Social Reintegration in South Africa', in Cilliers (ed.), *Dismissed*, pp. 111–27.
[58] See William Shawcross, *Cambo-*

dia's New Deal (Washington DC: Carnegie Endowment for International Peace, 1994), Chapter 3.
[59] *Ibid.*, p. 72.
[60] Interview with Col. Ghobashi, Chief Military Observer (ONUMOZ), 8 February 1994.
[61] 'Final Report of the Secretary-General on the UN Operation in Mozambique', S/1994/1449, 23 December 1994, paras 15 and 36; and Stephen, 'Demobilisation in Mozambique'.
[62] 'Mutiny Ruffles Mozambique's Fragile Peace', *The Guardian*, 3 March 1995. See also Alex Vines, *Angola and Mozambique: The Aftermath of Conflict*, Conflict Studies 280 (London: Research Institute for the Study of Conflict and Terrorism, 1995), pp. 19–20.
[63] Motumi and Hudson, 'Rightsizing', p. 114.
[64] *Ibid.*, p. 126.
[65] Cock, 'The Social Integration of Demobilised Soldiers', p. 13.
[66] See Ginifer, *Managing Arms in Peace Processes: Rhodesia/Zimbabwe*, pp. 50–51.
[67] Rupiah, 'Demobilisation and Integration', p. 59.
[68] See 'Statement of Steven Fanning' in Weiland and Braham (eds), *The Namibian Peace Process*, p. 108. For the problems associated with *Koevoet*, see p. 113.
[69] *Ibid.*, p. 108.
[70] 'El Salvador Moves Towards Reconciliation', *UN Chronicle*, vol. 31, no. 4, December 1994, p. 25.
[71] Dessables was quoted in 'Haiti Pins Future on Police, Courts', *Washington Post*, 1 February 1995.
[72] de Soto and del Castillo, 'Implementation of Comprehensive Peace Agreements', p. 189.
[73] For the attempts to legislate and define the future role of the secret

services in post-apartheid South Africa, see Kevin A. O'Brien, 'South Africa's New Intelligence Environment', in Jakkie Cilliers and Markus Reichardt (ed.), *About Turn: The Transformation of the South African Military and Intelligence* (Pretoria: Institute for Defence Policy, 1995), pp. 170–91.

[74] For an elaboration of these proposals, see Nicole Ball, 'Reducing Military Expenditure in Africa', Paper prepared for Global Coalition for Africa, April 1992.

[75] See Rocky Williams, 'Between a Rock and a Hard Place: Morality and the Development of a Professional Military Ethic', *African Security Review*, vol. 4, no. 3, 1995, pp. 3–24.

[76] Robert D'A Henderson, 'South African Intelligence under De Klerk', in Cilliers and Reichardt (eds), *About Turn*, pp. 158–59.

[77] *Ibid.*, p. 164.

[78] Quoted in O'Brien, 'South Africa's New Intelligence Environment', p. 187. For a discussion of 'third force violence' after the transition see, Robert D'A. Henderson, 'South African Intelligence Transition from de Klerk to Mandela: An Update', *International Journal of Intelligence and Counter Intelligence*, vol. 8, no. 4, Winter 1994, pp. 471–85.

[79] 'Report of the Joint Group for the Investigation of Politically Motivated Illegal Armed Groups in El Salvador', Annex to S/1994/989, 22 October 1994, p. 15.

[80] Personal interviews with MICIVH and UNMIH officials in Haiti, May 1995.

[81] 'Concern over Death Squads', *Latin America Monitor*, vol. 11, no. 7, July 1994, p. 9.

[82] de Soto and del Castillo, 'Implementation of Comprehensive Peace Agreements', p. 189.

Chapter IV

[1] 'Third Progress Report of the Secretary-General on the UN Observer Mission in Liberia', S/1994/463, 18 April 1994, para. 29; see also S/1994/760, 24 June 1994, para. 14.

[2] See 'Mutinies Endanger Maputo Peace Plans', *Daily Telegraph*, 29 July 1994.

[3] See the excellent article by Virginia Page Fortna, 'Success and Failure in Southern Africa: Peacekeeping in Namibia and Angola', in Bradd Hayes and Daniel Daniel (eds), *Beyond Traditional Peacekeeping* (London: Macmillan, 1995), pp. 282–99.

[4] See 'Twelfth Progress Report of the Secretary-General on the UN Observer Mission in Liberia', S/1995/781, 9 September 1995, para. 41.

[5] For a fuller discussion of this issue, see Mats R. Berdal, *Whither UN Peacekeeping?*, Adelphi Paper 281 (London: Brassey's for the IISS, 1993), p. 68.

[6] For an account of CFM activities, see Brigadier J. H. Learmont, 'Reflections from Rhodesia', *RUSI Journal*, vol. 125, no. 4, December 1980.

[7] IISS, 'Integration and Demobilisation in South Africa', *Strategic Comments*, vol. 1, no. 6, July 1995.

[8] It is worth noting that the reluctance of many countries and donors to invest in security sector reform has opened for growing private sector involvement, often of a dubious nature. See 'Training the Guns', *Africa Confidential*, vol. 36, no. 21, 20 October 1995.

[9] Ginifer, *Managing Arms in Peace Processes: Rhodesia/Zimbabwe*, p. 54.

[10] *Ibid.*

[11] Kühne, Weimer and Fandrych (eds), *International Workshop on the Successful Conclusion of the United Nations Operations in Mozambique*,

p. 14.
[12] *Demobilisation and Reintegration in Africa*, para. 74
[13] Kühne, Weimer and Fandrych (eds), *International Workshop on the Successful Conclusion of the United Nations Operations in Mozambique*, p. 22.
[14] See *Improving the Prospects for Future International Peace Operations*, Office of Technology Assessment (Washington DC: US Government Printing Office, September 1995). For the different categories of sensors, see especially pp. 106–8.
[15] Milton Finger, 'Technologies to Support Peacekeeping Operations', in *Ibid.*, pp. 105–8.
[16] 'Further Report of the Secretary-General on the United Nations Angola Verification Mission (UNAVEM II)', S/24858, 25 November 1992, para. 47.
[17] S/24145, 24 June 1992, para. 35, and Berdal, *Whither UN Peacekeeping?*, pp. 37–39.
[18] Meetings and interviews with: ONUMOZ staff, Mozambique, February 1994; officers of the Bangladeshi ONUMOZ contingent in Nampula, northern Mozambique, February 1994; and UNMIH staff, Haiti, May 1995.
[19] 'Report of the Secretary-General on Stand-by Arrangements for Peace-keeping', S/1995/943, 10 November 1995.
[20] *Ibid.*
[21] *Ibid.*
[22] Anthony McDermott, *United Nations Financing Problems and the New Generation of Peacekeeping and Peace Enforcement*, Occasional Paper 16 (Brown, RI: Thomas J. Watson Institute, 1994), p. 1.
[23] *UNIDIR Newsletter*, nos 28–29, December 1994–May 1995, pp. 45–50. See also *UNDP Human Develop-ment Report 1994* (Oxford: Oxford University Press, 1994).
[24] *Africa Confidential*, vol. 23, no. 23, 19 November 1993. See also Patrick M. Blagden, 'Mine Clearance', *UNIDIR Newsletter*, nos 28–29, December 1994–May 1995, p. 20.
[25] 'Land-mines', *Africa Research Bulletin*, vol. 31, no. 1, 1994.
[26] Blagden, 'Mine Clearance', p. 21. For some of the new technologies, see *Improving the Prospects for Future International Peace Operations*, pp. 99–104 and 108–10.
[27] Existing restrictions are governed by the 'UN Convention on Prohibi-tions or Restrictions on the Use of Certain Conventional Weapons which may be Deemed to be Excessively Injurious or to Have Indiscriminate Effects', adopted in 1980. For its obvious weaknesses, see *Landmines Must be Stopped: ICRC Special Brochure*, September 1995, p. 60.
[28] For an indication of some of the problems with 'half-measures', see *ibid.*, p. 45.
[29] 'Further Report of the Secretary-General on the UN Observer Mission in El Salvador', S/26790, 23 November 1993, para. 63.
[30] *Ibid.*, para. 65.
[31] de Soto and del Castillo, 'Imple-mentation of Comprehensive Peace Agreements', p. 189. The fears expressed in this article have not been assuaged by developments since the departure of the UN mission. Private interviews, New York, April 1996.
[32] *Demobilisation and Reintegration in Africa*, para. 65.
[33] S/26790, 23 November 1993, para. 78.
[34] *Ibid.*, para. 68.
[35] World Bank Discussion Meeting, Washington DC, June 1994.
[36] Colletta and Ball, 'War to Peace Transition in Uganda', p. 39, and

'Development Aid for Military Reform: A Pathway to Peace', *Policy Focus,* No. 6, ODC, Washington DC, 1993.
[37] Alvaro de Soto and Graciana del Castillo, 'Obstacles to Peacebuilding', *Foreign Policy,* no. 94, Spring 1994, p. 70.
[38] *Ibid.,* p. 72.
[39] See Susan Willett, 'Ostriches, Wise Old Elephants and Economic Reconstruction in Mozambique', *International Peacekeeping,* vol. 2, no. 1, Spring 1995, pp. 34–55. See also Ramesh Srivastava, *Reintegrating Demobilised Combatants: The Role of Small Enterprise Development* (Geneva: ILO, 1995), p. 4.
[40] The point is also made by de Soto and del Castillo, who argue that 'flexibility may also be needed in supporting unconventional institutional reforms establishing peace-oriented national governance'. See 'Obstacles to Peacebuilding', p. 80.
[41] *Governance: The World Bank's Experience (Executive Summary),* Operations Policy Department, the World Bank, Washington DC, 1991.
[42] Articles of Agreement, Article III, Section 5(b). For a fuller discussion of the World Bank's governance-related activities, see *Governance.*
[43] *Ibid.*
[44] The World Bank insists that its concern with 'accountability, transparency and the rule of law ... is exclusively with the contribution they make to social and economics development'.
[45] del Castillo, 'Arms-for-Land Deal'.
[46] For an elaboration of this and related suggestions see, de Soto and del Castillo, 'Obstacles to Peacebuilding', pp. 79–80.
[47] See Rosemary Righter, *Utopia Lost: The United Nations and World Order* (New York: The Twentieth Century Fund Press, 1995), chapters 1 and 2.
[48] The World Bank defines low-income countries as those with a GNP per capita of $610 or less in 1990. See *Adjustment in Africa: Reforms, Results, and the Road Ahead* (Oxford: Oxford University Press for the World Bank, 1994), p. xvii.
[49] Peter Utting, 'Linking Peace and Rehabilitation in Cambodia', in Utting (ed.), *Between Hope and Insecurity: The Social Consequences of the Cambodian Peace Process* (Geneva: UNRISD, 1994), p. 9.
[50] E. V. K. FitzGerald, 'The Economic Dimension of Social Development and the Peace Process in Cambodia', in Utting (ed.), *Between Hope and Insecurity.*
[51] *Ibid.*
[52] Utting, 'Linking Peace and Rehabilitation in Cambodia', p. 9.

Conclusion

[1] Stephen J. Stedman, 'UN Intervention in Civil Wars: Imperatives of Choice and Strategy', in Daniel and Hayes (ed.), *Beyond Traditional Peacekeeping.*
[2] I. William Zartman (ed.), *Collapsed States: The Disintegration and Restoration of Legitimate Authority* (London: Lynne Rienner, 1995), p. 1.
[3] Drawing upon the African experience, Zartman notes the inherent difficulty of trying to 'establish an absolute threshold of collapse'.